ATLA BIBLIOGRAPHY SERIES
edited by Dr. Kenneth E. Rowe

1. *A Guide to the Study of the Holiness Movement*, by Charles Edwin Jones. 1974.
2. *Thomas Merton: A Bibliography*, by Marquita E. Breit. 1974.
3. *The Sermon on the Mount: A History of Interpretation and Bibliography*, by Warren S. Kissinger, 1975.
4. *The Parables of Jesus: A History of Interpretation and Bibliography*, by Warren S. Kissinger. 1979.

HOMOSEXUALITY and the JUDEO–CHRISTIAN TRADITION

An annotated bibliography

TOM HORNER

ATLA Bibliography Series, No. 5

The American Theological Library Assn.
The Scarecrow Press, Inc.
Metuchen, N.J., & London
1981

Library of Congress Cataloging in Publication Data

Horner, Tom, 1927-
    Homosexuality and the Judeo-Christian tradition.

    (ATLA bibliography series ; no. 5)
    Includes indexes.
    1. Homosexuality and Christianity--Bibliography.
2. Homosexuality--Bibliography. I. Title. II. Series.
Z7164.S42H67 [BR115.H6]   016.2618'3576   81-899
ISBN 0-8108-1412-9   AACR2

CONTENTS

EDITOR'S NOTE

The American Theological Library Association Bibliography
Series is designed to stimulate and encourage the preparation
of reliable bibliographies and guides to the literature of religious studies in all of its scope and variety. Compilers
are free to define their field, make their own selections, and
work out internal organization as the unique demands of the
subject require. We are pleased to publish Tom Horner's
annotated bibliography of homosexuality and the Judeo-Christian tradition as number 5 in our series.

Tom Horner holds the Ph.D. degree in religious studies from Columbia University and has done postdoctoral work
at the Ruprecht-Karl University in Heidelberg and at the
American School of Classical Studies in Athens. He is the
author of Sex in the Bible (Tuttle, 1974) and Jonathan Loved
David: Homosexuality in Biblical Times (Westminster, 1978)
and the translator of Gunkel's Psalms (Fortress, 1967), a
work that is now in its sixth printing.

Kenneth E. Rowe, Editor

Drew University Library
Madison, New Jersey 07940

PREFACE

Numerous church bodies today are discussing homosexuality
in one connection or another: church conferences and study
commissions are debating the issue; theological seminaries
are addressing the subject in their curriculum; students are
writing term papers on the theme; lay persons are seeking
information on what was heretofore an unmentionable subject.
Resources to support such study and reflection from a wide
variety of disciplines are difficult to locate. Although several
preliminary lists have been made available (see Part IV below), no comprehensive, annotated bibliography has appeared
that deals with homosexuality within the framework of the
Jewish and Christian traditions. This bibliography aims to
fill that need.

First, however, a word about what this bibliography
is not. It is not a listing of all primary sources on homosexuality in the entire history of the Jewish and Christian
traditions, examples of which would be the remarks of a
first-century Philo Judaeus or the historian Josephus against
certain expressions of homosexuality. Readers may find the
most relevant data in regard to these two early figures in
Derrick Sherwin Bailey's Homosexuality and the Western
Christian Tradition or Vern L. Bullough's Sexual Variance
in Society and History (both of which are listed here). Other
historical data will, likewise, be found in modern works that
are relevant to the particular subject.

The major primary source for the subject of homosexuality in the Judeo-Christian tradition is, of course, the Bible,
though scripture is hardly preoccupied with the subject. For

the biblical authors homosexuality was not an area of major
concern. One has to be practically a specialist--or know
how to use one's concordance very well--even to find all the
relevant texts. For this reason I have added an appendix to
this bibliography listing principal biblical references. And
yet what concern that has been expressed over the years in
regard to these references has come about largely because
of the way or ways that they have been understood--or mis-
understood. Therefore books and articles that discuss the
biblical references constitute an important part of this bibliography. Exceptions are biblical commentaries. It would
serve no useful purpose to list every commentary that has
ever commented on a homosexual reference, though readers
doing biblical research should look up the relevant texts in
their favorite commentaries. Those in the Anchor Bible series (Doubleday) and the Old and New Testament Library (Westminster) are highly recommended as starting points.

In addition to biblical materials I have included modern works that illuminate the subject of homosexuality in the
Jewish and Christian traditions. There have been two gay-
liberation movements in modern times. The first one began
in 1869 with the coining of the word "homosexual" by a Hun-
garian scholar named Benkert (who wrote under the name
of Kertbeny). The word appeared in a tract that protested
the proposal of some anti-homosexual legislation in Prussia
that was pending at the time. The legislation was passed in
1871. Although a protest movement of sorts had already be-
gun about 1863 in Germany, Dr. Benkert's tract marked the
beginning of a significant literary output that flourished in
England and on the Continent, particularly in Germany. This
movement came to an end with Hitler's purges and concentration camps well before the advent of World War II. The
second gay-liberation movement began in 1969, when gay pa-
trons in a Greenwich Village bar offered resistance during
what was then considered only a routine police raid. What
has happened since then is well known. It is largely this
second phase of the movement that has spurred the publication of the majority of titles in this bibliography, including
most pro-homosexual literature that has come from within
the churches themselves (example: Towards a Quaker View
of Sex) or from Christians speaking quite independently of
their church bodies (example: Norman Pittenger's Time for
Consent). Because it was a forbidden topic for so long the
proliferation of books may be accounted for by a feeling of
trying to make up for lost time. This in turn has sparked
significant anti-homosexual literature, which is also repre-
sented here.

This bibliography does not aspire to completeness. Resources that will not be found here are: newspaper accounts, items from newsletters of the various gay caucuses, articles from religious periodicals that are of minor importance, book reviews and book-review articles, audiovisual resources, and foreign-language works not available in English translation. However, many books and articles listed here-- including one major bibliography--include foreign-language sources within their particular contexts. Researchers who read the other languages will want to seek these out. But, because this guide is designed primarily for pastors, seminarians, and lay persons who do not use the other languages, I have not included them here.

The bibliographical description of each item is designed to use as few cryptic abbreviations as possible. I have not included prices since they are subject to change. Nor do I indicate whether a book is available in paperback. Far more important than the description, however, is the annotation that follows most entries. The few items without annotations were ones that the author was unable to examine personally. My aim in the annotations is to describe briefly but accurately the work and its relevance to the study of homosexuality from a Judeo-Christian point of view and to refrain from value judgments. Such a task is not an easy one. In the final analysis I can only hope that enough has been said about the book or article to help users select the materials they need to make their own critical evaluation. My principal aim is to connect the user with the principal available resources.

I would like to thank Dr. Paul Meacham, Senior Editor of the Westminster Press, and Dr. Louie Crew, Associate Professor of English at the University of Wisconsin, Stevens Point, for recommending me to do the project, and Dr. Kenneth E. Rowe, Editor of the American Theological Library Association's Bibliography Series and his committee, for their help and faith in my ability to complete the project. It is really not complete, as both they and I know. But let us hope that it can at least serve as a good starting point for students and others in compiling their own bibliographies for their particular areas of research.

Tom Horner

New Orleans
September 1980

HOMOSEXUALITY AND THE JUDEO-CHRISTIAN TRADITION

I. BOOKS

1. Adair, Nancy, and Casey Adair, eds. Word Is Out: Stories of Some of Our Lives. San Francisco: New Glide, 1978; rpt., New York: Dell/Delta, 1978.

   Highly personal accounts of the lives of gay persons, from college students to senior citizens, all of whom feel quite good about themselves as they are. The well-known activist Sally Gearhart comments how the Judeo-Christian tradition overlooks some of its own gay content.

2. Altman, Dennis. Homosexual: Oppression and Liberation. New York: Outerbridge & Lazard, 1971; rpt., New York: Avon, 1973.

   One of the first major theoretical works on homosexual liberation. There are references to Christainity throughout the first half of the book, and to Judaism and homosexuality on pages 56, 75 and 146 (reprint pagination).

3. Baars, Conrad. The Homosexual's Search for Happiness. Chicago: Franciscan Herald, 1977.

4. Babuscio, Jack. We Speak for Ourselves: Experiences in Homosexual Counseling. Philadelphia: Fortress, 1977.

Case studies of seventy confessed homosexual persons --married, parental, jailed, religious, secret, guilt-ridden, youthful, aged, professional, famous, contented. Uniformly the attitude is sympathetic. Aimed at clinical counselors and pastors. Contains bibliography.

5. Bahnsen, Greg L. Homosexuality: A Biblical View. Grand Rapids, Michigan: Baker, 1978.

In this 152-page paperback a professor of apologetics and ethics at the Reformed Theological Seminary, Jackson, Mississippi, says that scripture forbids homosexuality and that this is unequivocal. It is not only a sin, he says, but a crime and should be forbidden by law. He also advocates discrimination in housing and employment. Footnotes are limited to scriptural references, but there is a bibliography.

6. Bailey, Derrick Sherwin. Common Sense About Sexual Ethics: A Christian View. New York: Macmillan, 1962.

7. _____. Homosexuality and the Western Christian Tradition. London: Longmans, Green, 1955; rpt., Hamden, Connecticut: Shoestring, 1975.

Bailey is quite thorough in his treatment of homosexuality in the 2,000-year history of the Christian Church. Other than that, the book's unique feature was its original contention that the Sodom story represents only the sin of inhospitality and has nothing to do with intended homosexual rape. The book contributed significantly to the decriminalization of homosexuality in Great Britain.

8. _____. Sexual Relation in Christian Thought. New York: Harper, 1959.

9. Bailey, Paul Joseph. An Analysis of the Utilization of Organization Rhetoric: The United Church of Christ's Rhetorical Construction of Postures Towards Homosexuality. Doctoral dissertation, Penn State University, 1978.

This dissertation attempts to show how a denomination used rhetoric to stall a decision on an issue. However, since Bailey's thesis was written the United Church of Christ made the decision (in 1979) to ordain homosexual candidates for its ministry.

10. Barnett, Walter. Sexual Freedom and the Constitution: An Inquiry into the Constitutionality of Repressive Sex Laws. Albuquerque: University of New Mexico Press, 1973.

Chapters 6 and 7 summarize the scientific knowledge about homosexuality up to 1972. See the same author's Homosexuality and the Bible: An Interpretation, No. 408, below.

11. Barnhouse, Ruth Tiffany. Homosexuality: A Symbolic Confusion. New York: Seabury, 1977.

This work considers homosexuality from both the scientific and theological perspective, these two modes being seen, in the last analysis, as inseparable. Barnhouse presents the view that homosexuality is not only an alternative lifestyle but also a developmental failure.

12. _____, and Urban T. Holmes III, eds. Male and Female: Christian Approaches to Sexuality. New York: Seabury, 1976.

A collection of essays on various aspects of sexuality, including four on homosexuality: "Homosexuality: An Overview," by Alan Bell; "Homosexuality Is Not Just an Alternative Life Style," by Charles W. Socarides; "A Theological Approach to Homosexuality," by Norman Pittenger; and "Some Words of Caution," by William Muehl. Those by Pittinger and Bell are positive on the subject; the other two are negative.

13. Barth, Karl. Church Dogmatics. Volume III, Part 4. Edinburgh: T.&T. Clark, 1961.

This is where to find Barth's ethical position on homosexuality. He sees it as both sin (disobedience) and unnatural (a perversion of the created order).

14. Batchelor, Edward, ed. Homosexuality and Ethics. New York: Pilgrim, 1980.

 The thoughts expressed in this collection of essays range from total condemnation of homosexuality to acceptance of homosexual acts as natural and good. Protestant, Catholic, and Jewish points of view are explored. Contributors: Roger Shinn, Tom Driver, Gregory Baum, Rosemary Ruether, Ruth Barnhouse, Charles Curran, Norman Pittenger, Robert Gordis, Neale Secor, James Nelson, Lisa Cahill, and others.

15. Bell, Alan P., and Martin S. Weinberg. Homosexualities: A Study of Diversity Among Men and Women. New York: Simon and Schuster, 1978.

 This book is an official publication of the Institute for Sex Research, founded by the late Alfred C. Kinsey, whose earlier volumes on sexuality also treated homosexuality but not to the extent that this one does in regard to religion. The chapter "Religiousness" in Part III, pages 149-154, discusses the attitudes of those interviewed toward organized religion.

16. Berton, Pierre. The Comfortable Pew. Philadelphia: Lippincott, 1965.

 Berton chides the churches for their tendency to "cast out the outcasts," with homosexuals at the top of the list: "A very good case can be made that the homosexual is the modern equivalent of the leper."

17. Bieber, Irving. Homosexuality: A Psychoanalytic Study. New York: Basic Books, 1962.

 Though this book does not concern itself with the issue of homosexuality and the Judeo-Christian tradition, it is included here because it is the basic text treating homosexuality as an illness and describing treatment for its cure. The work is based upon research with two control groups.

18. Borhek, Mary V. My Son Eric. New York: Pilgrim, 1979.

A true-life account of a mother, recently divorced
from her clergyman husband, who discovers that her
nineteen-year-old son is homosexual. The book documents her struggle and final acceptance of it. According to the book jacket, in the process "she discovers herself."

19. Boswell, John. Christianity, Social Tolerance, and Homosexuality: Gay People in Western Europe from the
Beginning of the Christian Era to the Fourteenth Century. Chicago: University of Chicago Press, 1980.

The unique feature here is Boswell's contention that
homosexuality was not singled out for derogation as
"unnatural" until the thirteenth century, when it became associated with certain heretical movements,
largely through historical accident. All will not agree,
though many are calling this "the definitive work" on
homosexuality in the historical realm.

20. Boyd, Malcolm. Am I Running with You, God? Garden
City, New York: Doubleday, 1977.

Episcopal priest and civil-rights and antiwar activist
transforms himself into a gay activist. An earlier
work with a similar title (Are You Running with Me,
Jesus?), although not a gay book, included one reference to a gay bar.

21. _____. Take Off the Masks. Garden City, New
York: Doubleday, 1978.

The well-known nightclub Episcopal priest presents
here another segment of his autobiography, this time
describing in detail his homosexuality. The work is
noteworthy for its frankness.

22. Brewster, Ralph H. Six Thousand Beards of Athos.
London: Hogarth, 1935.

23. Brill, Earl. The Christian Moral Vision. New York:
Seabury, 1979.

24. Brown, Arthur A. The Philosophical Assumptions Un-
     derlying Homosexuality: A Frame of Reference for
     Advisors to Students. Doctoral dissertation, Boston
     College, 1977.

25. Brown, Howard. Familiar Faces, Hidden Lives: The
     Story of Homosexual Men in America Today. New
     York: Harcourt Brace Jovanovich, 1976.

     Chapter 10, "Religion," pages 159-179, is in fact al-
     most entirely a discussion of attitudes toward homo-
     sexuality within the Judeo-Christian tradition, more
     especially the Jewish, although the author also dis-
     cusses his own Methodist background. The book, use-
     ful in other respects as well, is actually addressed to
     the heterosexual reader.

26. Bryant, Anita. The Anita Bryant Story: The Survival
     of Our Nation's Families and the Threat of Militant
     Homosexuality. Old Tappan, New Jersey: Revell,
     1977.

     This chronicles the beginnings of Bryant's opposition
     to what she calls "militant homosexuality" in Dade
     County, Florida, and presents her side of the issue
     in the referendum that was held there in June 1977.
     The book is an interesting documentation of a strictly
     fundamentalist view and use of scripture in the homo-
     sexual debate.

27. _____. Save Our Children. Old Tappan, New Jer-
     sey: Revell, 1978.

     This book is a follow-up to The Anita Bryant Story.
     It is an account of Bryant's political and religious ef-
     forts to resist the relaxation of restrictions on homo-
     sexuality. She presents here the views that lead her
     to regard homosexuality as a social, religious, and
     familial danger.

28. Buckley, Michael J. Morality and the Homosexual: A
     Catholic Approach to a Moral Problem. London and
     Glasgow: Sands, 1959.

A handbook for priests, Catholic moral theologians, and psychiatric practitioners that is designed to outline the teachings of the Roman Catholic Church on the issue at the time. The conclusion is that homosexuality is an unnatural condition that must and can be changed.

29. Bullough, Vern L. Homosexuality: A History. New York: New American Library, 1979.

Everything is covered, in brief, from ancient Greece to the modern gay-liberation movement. Chapter 2, "Religion and Homosexuality," begins with the early Jewish and Christian attitudes, includes what some medieval theologians had to say, and ends with a statement from the Reverend Troy Perry, founder of the Metropolitan Community Church.

30. _____. Sexual Variance in Society and History. New York: Wiley, 1976.

This is a major contribution to the literature of sexuality, especially homosexuality. The author has published several smaller books with similar titles but none of them has the scope and depth of this one. Some sample chapters: "The Jewish Contribution," "Roman Mythology and Reality," "Classical Sources of Christian Hostility to Sex," and so on, for 715 pages.

31. _____, and Bonnie Bullough. Sin, Sickness, and Sanity: A History of Sexual Attitudes. New York: New American Library, 1977.

The relevant material here is found in Chapters 2 and 3: "Why the Hostility to Sex?" and "Unnatural Sex." The authors say that the ascetic values of Stoicism exerted a powerful influence on early Christianity. They discuss sex-negative attitudes in the Christian churches from the beginning through modern times.

32. Carpenter, Edward, ed. Ioläus: An Anthology of Friendship. New York: Mitchell Kennerley, 1917.

A collection of direct literary quotations from the Bible

to Whitman illustrating close (mostly male) personal friendships, including the medieval Christian period, when such friendships were "socially denied and ignored" but nevertheless flourished, this book was an important influence among pro-homosexual advocates for many years.

33. Cavanaugh, John R. Counseling the Homosexual. Huntington, Indiana: Our Sunday Visitor, 1977.

34. _____. Counseling the Invert. Milwaukee: Bruce, 1966.

   Traditional viewpoint.

35. Church of England. Board for Social Responsibility. Homosexual Relationships: A Contribution to the Discussion. London: Church Information Office, 1979.

   A working party set up by the Board for Social Responsibility examines the claim that those who are homosexual should be accorded the same respect and freedom as exists for heterosexuals, and the extent to which that claim can find backing in Christian terms. The conclusion of the working party is that marriage remains the norm for human sexual relationships, but that "there are circumstances in which individuals may justifiably choose to enter into a homosexual relationship."

36. Churchill, Wainright. Homosexual Behavior Among Males: A Cross-Cultural and Cross-Species Investigation. New York: Hawthorn, 1967; rpt., Englewood Cliffs, New Jersey: Prentice-Hall, 1971.

   Chapter 4, "The Cross-Cultural Data," is a brief delineation of homosexual acceptance or rejection in several cultures, ancient and modern. The rejection by the Persian-Zoroastrian tradition, Churchill says, represents the most extreme stand against homosexuality in history and was of great influence upon the Judeo-Christian tradition.

37. Clark, Don. Loving Someone Gay. Millbrae, California: Celestial Arts, 1977; rpt., New York: New American Library, 1978.

There is very little on religion or the Church in this book, but because its entire thrust is toward helping those who are troubled by homosexuality or helping those who work with those who are troubled by it, its availability should be noted. There are two pages (218-219 in the reprint) devoted to the clergy as counselors to homosexual persons.

38. Cole, William G. Sex and Love in the Bible. London: Hodder and Stoughton, 1960.

In earlier chapters Cole reviews the sexual background of the ancient world. In Chapter 10, "Homosexuality in the Bible," he deals with the more important scriptural references. He sees homosexual persons as "sick" but urges Christians at least to stop being moralistic on the subject.

39. _____. Sex in Christianity and Psychoanalysis. New York: Oxford University Press, 1955.

40. Coleman, Peter. Christian Attitudes to Homosexuality. London: SPCK, 1980.

Contains an account of the development of medical and psychological views; a review of the biblical texts and their interpretation both past and present; a historical survey of Christian attitudes; and an account of the shift in the Christian ethical judgment from hostility to tolerance and acceptance.

41. Collins, Gary R., ed. The Secrets of Our Sexuality: Role Liberation for the Christian. Waco, Texas: Word Books, 1976.

The relevant chapter here is "A Biblical View of Homosexuality," in which conservative scholar and college president Dennis F. Kinlaw presents a systematic

defense of the Church's traditional views against homosexuality on biblical grounds.

42. Davidson, Alex. The Returns of Love: A Contemporary
    View of Homosexuality. Downers Grove, Illinois:
    Inter-Varsity, 1970.

    Through a series of letters a young man shares with
    a friend his agonies and conflicts as a homosexual
    Christian. He yearns for same-sex love and sexual
    fulfillment but is persuaded that for him, as a Chris-
    tian, the only answer lies in control and celibacy.

43. Diamond, Liz. The Lesbian Primer. Salem, Massa-
    chusetts: Women's Educational Media, 1979.

    This is a book to make women who are homosexual
    feel good about being so. Only one part of Chapter 5,
    "Myth-Conceptions," deals with religion: it is myth-
    conception #1 that "lesbianism is against religion."
    A few passages from the Bible are quoted, and read-
    ers are asked to draw their own conclusions.

44. Doherty, Dennis, ed. Dimensions of Human Sexuality.
    Garden City, New York: Doubleday, 1979.

    Prominent Roman Catholic scholars evaluate here the
    arguments and conclusions of the study Human Sexu-
    ality (see Kosnik et al., No. 105), which included
    homosexuality. They urge a new appreciation of sexu-
    ality as an expression of the total person.

45. Dover, K. J. Greek Homosexuality. Cambridge,
    Massachusetts: Harvard University Press, 1978; rpt.,
    New York: Random House, 1980.

    Strictly speaking, this book does not belong in this
    bibliography since it does not mention the Bible,
    Christians, or Jews. Nevertheless, it is the defini-
    tive work on Greek homosexuality, which is a part of
    the background of the New Testament world. It is
    included here as a basic reference in this area.

46. Drakeford, John W. A Christian View of Homosexuality. Nashville, Tennessee: Broadman, 1977.

This is a conservative and yet not entirely condemnatory approach by the director of the marriage and family counseling center of the Southwest Baptist Theological Seminary. Drakeford regards homosexuality as sin and argues that, while there is no cure, homosexuals may alter their behavior somewhat by means of what he calls "Integrity Therapy" and with the loving support of the Church.

47. _____. Forbidden Love. Waco, Texas: Word Books, 1971.

48. Eglinton, J. Z. [pseud.]. Greek Love. New York: Oliver Layton, 1964.

Boy-love (pederasty) from ancient Greece to modern times. Extensive notes, bibliography. 504 pages.

49. Enroth, Ronald M., and Gerald E. Johnson. The Gay Church. Grand Rapids, Michigan: Eerdmans, 1974.

"Homosexuals constitute perhaps the largest minority group in America, and they are no longer a silent minority," state the authors. Hence the mainline churches must take a stance toward them. The stance of this book is negative: a fundamentalist polemic.

50. Epstein, Louis M. Sex Laws and Customs in Judaism. New York: Bloch, 1948; rev. ed., New York: KTAV, 1968.

This scholarly work shows no acceptance of homosexuality but is nevertheless quite good in pointing out the progressive development of the Old Testament laws pertaining to it. It also stresses the use of the Hebrew noun to'ebah ("abomination") as a reference primarily to idolatry.

51. Evans, Arthur. Witchcraft and the Gay Counterculture. Boston: Fag Rag Books, 1978.

Witches, Celts, and American Indians are eulogized while Christians, Romans, and all capitalists are excoriated in this overview of Western history written from the standpoint of the mother-goddess cult. The book's approach is admittedly one-sided and, to put it bluntly, revolutionary.

52. Evening, Margaret. Who Walk Alone. Downers Grove, Illinois: Inter-Varsity, 1974.

Speaks highly of the gifts, sensitivity, and loving natures characterizing many homosexual persons. "We can thus accept with humility the special gifts mediated to us through those who are His homosexual children, our brothers and sisters whom we cannot and would not disown."

53. Fairchild, Betty, and Nancy Hayward. Now That You Know: What Every Parent Should Know About Homosexuality. New York: Harcourt Brace Jovanovich, 1979.

As the subtitle suggests, the book is addressed particularly to parents who learn that a son or daughter is homosexual. Chapter 7, "Gays and Religion," deals with both the Jewish and Christian positions in regard to homosexuality and attempts to show that they need not be interpreted as condemnatory. Bibliography.

54. Fone, Byrne H. S. Hidden Heritage: History and the Gay Imagination, An Anthology. New York: Avocation, 1979.

This comprehensive volume consists of primary texts, whole or in part, drawn from Plato to the present. After the introductory ancient material, there is a brief section illustrating a Christian reaction, followed by selections showing the survival of the Greek ideal in the Middle Ages and its rejuvenation in the Renaissance. The longest section of the book covers the eighteenth and nineteenth centuries. Index and bibliography are lacking.

55. Foster, Jeannette. Sex Variant Women in Literature:
     A Historical and Quantitative Survey. New York:
     Vantage, 1956; 2d ed., with an Afterword by Barbara
     Grier, Baltimore: Diana, 1975.

     The significance of Foster's work for this list is her
     advocacy of a lesbian relationship in the story of Ruth
     (between Ruth and Naomi). The book of Ruth, she
     says, "is the first of a thin line of delicate portray-
     als ... of an attachment which, however innocent, is
     nevertheless still basically variant."

56. Foucault, Michel. The History of Sexuality. Vol. I.
     Trans. by Robert Hurley. New York: Pantheon,
     1978; rpt., New York: Vintage, 1980.

     This first volume of a proposed multivolume work
     deals with sexual oppression as politically motivated
     and says that this is a relatively recent phenomenon--
     that is, going back only to the seventeenth century.
     As this (French) author sees it, "the powers that be"
     employ many forms of sexual oppression, including
     the suppression of homosexuality, to keep the citizenry
     under control.

57. Furnish, Victor Paul. The Moral Teaching of Paul:
     Selected Issues. Nashville, Tennessee: Abingdon,
     1979.

     Homosexuality is one of four issues discussed by Paul
     that are also topics of discussion in the churches to-
     day. Pages 52-83 are devoted to this issue. Furnish
     says that Paul knew only of the exploitative type of ho-
     mosexuality, and this is the only sort that he is con-
     demning. Indispensable for those researching the
     Apostle Paul.

58. Gangel, Kenneth. The Gospel and the Gay. Nashville,
     Tennessee: Nelson, 1978.

     Despite the title, this book devotes far more space to
     the Old Testament than to the New. Gangel's conclu-
     sion is that homosexuals are made, not born. He in-

cludes an interview with a young man "who had been rescued by God from a tragic involvement with homosexuality."

59. Garde, Noel I. Jonathan to Gide: The Homosexual in History. New York: Vantage, 1964.

Beginning with the biblical Jonathan, this work includes brief biographical sketches of all the "greats" who were homosexual or alleged to have been homosexual throughout history. 757 pages.

60. Gearhart, Sally, and William R. Johnson, eds. Loving Women/Loving Men: Gay Liberation and the Church. San Francisco: Glide, 1974.

A collection of essays, including one on the ordination of William R. Johnson, first avowed homosexual candidate to be ordained by one of the mainline denominations. Scripture analysis by Robert Treese says the Sodom story may not refer to homosexuality. The collection includes gay-related church history to 1973.

61. Gerassi, John. The Boys of Boise: Furor, Vice, and Folly in an American City. New York: Macmillan, 1966.

A sociological study that describes the atmosphere of a small town, Boise, Idaho, which was the site of a homosexual scandal and "witch hunt" in 1955. The depth of the scandal reveals the inner workings of a small town and its morality--or lack of it. Playing a leading role in the attack on gay men (women were not involved) was the Mormon Church in Boise.

62. Geyer, Marcia Lee. Human Rights or Homophobia? The Rising Tide. Los Angeles: Universal Fellowship, 1977.

Homophobia, a term coined by Dr. George Weinberg, is here defined as "prejudice against homosexuals." In this book Geyer investigates the nature and dynamics of homophobia and attempts to provide homosexual persons with a way to transform anger into understanding and understanding into "a Christ-like program of loving action."

63. Gibson, E. Lawrence. Get Off My Ship: Ensign Berg vs. the U.S. Navy. New York: Avon, 1978.

This book is about the trial of Ensign Vernon E. Berg III that resulted in his being discharged from the Navy for his homosexuality. Appendix B contains documents relating to the religious issue, namely testimonials and letters in his favor from John Boswell, Henri Nouwen, Robert McAfee Brown, Harvey Cox, Carter Heyward, Bishop Paul Moore, Jr., and many others.

64. Ginder, Richard. Binding with Briars: Sex and Sin in the Catholic Church. Englewood Cliffs, New Jersey: Prentice-Hall, 1975.

Fr. Ginder, a Roman Catholic priest, believes that the time is long overdue for a radical change in the attitudes of his church authorities on sexuality, including contraception, homosexuality, and celibacy. There is quite a strong criticism of the hierarchy, especially of the American hierarchy.

65. Goodich, Michael. The Unmentionable Vice: Homosexuality in the Late Medieval Period. Santa Barbara, California: ABC-Clio, 1979; rpt., Santa Barbara, California: Ross-Erikson, 1979.

Suggests that the systematic repression of homosexuality that took root in the eleventh century may be more representative of the Catholic Church's power struggle vis-à-vis the more liberal Greco-Roman ethos than of a true moralistic tradition. Copiously documented.

66. Gordis, Robert. Love and Sex: A Modern Jewish Perspective. New York: Farrar, Straus and Giroux, 1978.

Chapter 10, "Homosexuality and the Homosexual," is

the relevant one here. In theological language, Gordis says, "heterosexuality is the will of God ... homosexuality a violation of His will." It is an abnormality, an illness; nevertheless, "homosexuals deserve the same inalienable rights as do all their fellow human beings."

67. Graham, John. The Homosexual Kings of England. London: Tandem, 1968.

William Rufus, Richard Lion-heart, Edward II, James I (who sponsored the most famous version of the Bible in English), and others. Asserts, without any documentation, that William Rufus was killed in a jealous rage by his lover, William Tirel, Earl of Poix.

68. Graves, Robert. The White Goddess: A Historical Grammar of Poetic Myth. London: Faber & Faber, 1948; rpt., amended and enlarged ed., New York: Farrar, Straus and Giroux, 1966.

Graves several times mentions homosexuality in connection with the cult of the Great Mother (for him, "the White Goddess"), who had many elements of her worship incorporated into Christianity, especially in the cults of the saints. The brief index to this 492-page volume fails to indicate that there are numerous references in it to the Old Testament.

69. _____, and Raphael Patai. Hebrew Myths: The Book of Genesis. New York: McGraw-Hill, 1964.

The stories in Genesis are retold from the standpoint of all the ancient source material as well as the biblical text itself. Since a great deal of this material has to do with sexuality--and homosexuality--this book is important for researchers in this area. The format is the same as that of Graves's monumental two-volume work The Greek Myths.

70. Greene, Michael, David Holloway, and David Watson. The Church and Homosexuality: A Positive Answer to Current Questions. London: Hodder and Stoughton, 1980.

Despite the word "positive" in the subtitle, this work
is negative in its stance toward homosexuality. It is
a conservative reply to the recent Church of England
report (see No. 35).

71. Grey, Antony. Christian Society and the Homosexual.
     Oxford: Manchester College, 1966.

72. Gross, Alfred A. Strangers in Our Midst. Washington,
     D.C.: Public Affairs, 1962.

     Problems of the homosexual in American society from
     a religious standpoint. Considered somewhat radical
     at its time of publication.

73. Guidon, Andre. The Sexual Language: An Essay in
     Moral Theology. Ottawa: University of Ottawa Press,
     1976.

     The relevant chapter here is "Homosexuality," pages
     299-377.

74. Haeberle, Erwin J. The Sex Atlas. A New Illustrated
     Guide. New York: Seabury, 1978.

     This is a comprehensive one-volume survey of the
     whole range of human sexuality. It treats homosexu-
     ality as a normal form of sexual expression, just
     as it does heterosexuality. There is some treatment
     of the biblical references to both heterosexuality and
     homosexuality. The book is large-format and copiously
     illustrated and includes an extensive bibliography.
     There has been some criticism of the Episcopal Church
     press for having published this book.

75. Hamilton, Wallace. David at Olivet. New York: St.
     Martin's, 1979.

     A fictionalized version of the narrative of I-II Samuel,
     including David's having homosexual affairs with both
     Saul and Jonathan. As this author sees it, Saul's ex-
     treme jealousy of David stemmed from Saul's having

been a lover of the young Bethlehemite before the latter turned to Jonathan.

76. Hanckel, Frances, and John Cunningham. A Way of Love, a Way of Life: A Young Person's Introduction to What It Means to Be Gay. New York: Lothrop, Lee and Shepard, 1979.

Written for the young person who may have no knowledge of sex, the material covers the basics on the subject: e.g., "How to Tell If You're Gay," family relationships and friendships, and legal and medical aspects. There are references to religion throughout the book. Because it is thoroughly indexed, they may be found easily.

77. Hawkins, John Augustus. Attitudes Toward Sexual Involvement of Adults with Minors Among Certain Groups of Current and Former Theological School Students. Doctoral dissertation, Boston University, 1974.

78. Henry, George W. All the Sexes: A Study of Masculinity and Femininity. Foreword by David E. Roberts. New York: Holt, Rinehart and Winston, 1955.

The author discusses his thirty years of psychiatric research and observation of 9,000 cases, adding some psychological portraits drawn from literary analyses of such notables as David and Jonathan. Although there are several pages on sex in the Bible, readers should note that this material is found only in the 1955 edition of Dr. Henry's work--the paperback, issued by Macmillan in 1964, omitted it.

79. Hiltner, Seward. Sex Ethics and the Kinsey Reports. New York: Association, 1953.

80. Hoffman, Martin. The Gay World: Male Homosexuality and the Social Creation of Evil. New York: Basic Books, 1968.

81. Horner, Tom. Eros in Greece: A Sexual Inquiry. New

York: Privately printed, 1978.   (Available from author at 600 Frenchmen, New Orleans, LA   70116.)

Chapter 12, "Sex in Religion," or pages 104-111 in this 127-page paperback study of sexuality in modern Greece, discusses the attitudes of the Greek Orthodox Church toward homosexuality as well as other matters sexual.   Pointed out, though not particularly stressed, is the inconsistency between theory and practice in this regard.

82.   _____.   Jonathan Loved David: Homosexuality in Biblical Times.   Philadelphia: Westminster, 1978.

This book attempts to analyze all the biblical passages that deal with homosexuality, including those that some authors consider to deal with it but about which there is no universal agreement.   In regard to the latter, some reviewers caution that Horner's interpretation of the Jonathan-David liaison as a homosexual relationship is not convincing.   Extensive notes, suggested readings, and indexes.

83.   _____.   Sex in the Bible.   Rutland, Vermont, and Tokyo: Tuttle, 1974.

All the data relevant to the title are discussed briefly under twenty-four headings.   The book attempts to interpret the references only in context and to relate them to other passages of similar context.   The chapter on homosexuality is brief (twelve pages), but the subject is discussed briefly in other chapters as well. Scripture references are in the margins throughout.

84.   Hudson, Billy.   Christian Homosexuality.   North Hollywood, California: New Library Press, 1970.

85.   Humphreys, Laud.   Out of the Closets: The Sociology of Homosexual Liberation.   Englewood Cliffs, New Jersey: Prentice-Hall, 1972.

An Episcopal priest and educator outlines the movement, its causes, and development.   Some religious content.

86. _____. Tearoom Trade: Impersonal Sex in Public Places. Chicago: Aldine, 1970; expanded ed., 1975.

Sociological analysis of statistical data drawn from actual observation in a public men's room in St. Louis. The author also interviewed a number of the participants in regard to their need to engage in impersonal sex, family life, etc.

87. Hunt, Morton. Gay: What You Should Know About Homosexuality. New York: Farrar, Straus and Giroux, 1977; rpt., New York: Pocket Books, 1979.

Hunt, who has written previously on subjects for youth, provides an easy-to-read primer for young readers aged ten and up on what is known and not known about homosexuality. The book is neutral in tone. Pages 62-72 (of the paperback edition) discuss the traditional opposition to homosexuality in the Judeo-Christian tradition but point out how this attitude is undergoing challenge and change in today's society.

88. Hyde, H. Montgomery. The Other Love: An Historical and Contemporary Survey of Homosexuality in Britain. London: Heinemann, 1970.

The biblical and other ancient materials that affected the later British attitudes are reviewed on pages 29-32; the eighteenth-century clergyman and homosexuality, on pages 82-89; and the Church of England's Moral Welfare Council in social reform, on page 226. There is an allusion to The Jew of Malta, a play by Christopher Marlowe, on page 41.

89. Itkin, Mikhail. The Radical Jesus and Gay Consciousness. Long Beach, California: Communiversity West, 1972.

A hard-to-find monograph of approximately sixty pages. Not seen.

90. Jones, Clinton R. Homosexuality and Counseling. Philadelphia: Fortress, 1974.

The author offers advice on how to help homosexual persons "out of pain and toward fulfillment" as self-accepting and responsible individuals. Contains stories of case studies. Geared for the general reader as well as for pastors and counselors.

91. _____. Understanding Gay Relatives and Friends. New York: Seabury, 1978.

Here Jones writes as one "who believes that love is the central theme of the Gospel." There are case studies of a gay son, daughter, brother, sister, husband, wife, father, teacher, clergyman, transvestite husband, a transsexual son. Written in an engaging style, the book includes addresses of resource organizations and a bibliography.

92. _____. What About Homosexuality? Nashville, Tennessee: Nelson, 1972.

A rather brief paperback (86 pages) in which the noted canon at the Hartford Episcopal Cathedral presents a youth-forum-type introduction to the topic. It has been recommended for use in study groups.

93. Jones, M. Kimball. Toward a Christian Understanding of the Homosexual. New York: Association, 1966.

Jones suggests that for the true homosexual a setting that acts for the humanization of him- or herself can only exist in an encounter with another person of the same sex. Such an encounter is the only sexual setting in which the humanizing process can begin and then move on to become "a concrete and achievable reality."

94. Kamen, Henry. The Spanish Inquisition. New York: New American Library, 1965.

There is some discussion of sodomy in this general treatment of the Inquisition in Spain.

95. Kantrowitz, Arnie. Under the Rainbow: Growing Up

Gay. New York: Morrow, 1977; rpt., New York: Pocket Books, 1978.

References to Judaism are found throughout this gay autobiography. Boldly presented is the conflict between the pressures in Jewish family life toward conventionality and the author's desire to be himself. Yet he never hides his Jewishness and, once out, never his homosexuality.

96. Karlen, Arno. Sexuality and Homosexuality. New York: Norton, 1971.

Karlen's huge volume has been much praised by both reviewers and bibliographers for its detail and scope. Its treatment of the ancient Greek and biblical materials is limited, but this is still a useful tool on the whole subject of homosexuality. Modern case studies are interspersed with some of the historical material. Copiously footnoted.

97. Katz, Jonathan. Gay American History: Lesbians and Gay Men in the U.S.A. New York: Crowell, 1976; rpt., New York: Avon, 1978.

This book contains a great amount of information that is not to be found elsewhere in one volume: numerous primary documents of Roman Catholic missionaries describing homosexual practices among American Indians, cases of homosexual persecution in America, and so on. The 1063-page Avon edition contains 200 pages of notes and a fifty-seven-page index, under which see "Religion" for pertinent references.

98. Kelly, George A. The Political Struggle of Active Homosexuals to Gain Acceptance. Chicago: Franciscan Herald, 1975.

Favors civil but not ecclesiastical liberties. Chastity is still the ideal. 104 pages.

99. Keysor, Charles W., ed. What You Should Know About Homosexuality. Grand Rapids, Michigan: Zondervan, 1979.

There are six sections: homosexuality in the Old
Testament, in the New Testament, in the Church
fathers, and from the standpoints of psychology, the
law, and the Church. Five of the writers see homosexuality as forbidden by scripture and as intrinsically
wrong. The sixth--the psychiatrist--feels that homosexual persons have a problem of "psychological-
object choice" and can change.

100. Kiefer, Otto. Sexual Life in Ancient Rome. Trans.
by Gilbert and Helen Highet. London: Routledge and
Kegan Paul, 1934.

Includes all kinds of sexual information on ancient
Rome from the beginning to the time of the Emperor
Heliogabalus, including a discussion of the homosexu-
ality of Hadrian, Nero, Heliogabalus, and others.
There is some discussion of early Christian attitudes
toward matters sexual.

101. Kinsey, Alfred C., et al. Sexual Behavior in the Human Female. Philadelphia: Saunders, 1953.

Unlike the arrangement of Sexual Behavior in the Human Male, this volume scatters the religious data
throughout. On homosexuality and religious background see pages 463-466. In the index see page
numbers referring to "Jewish code" and "morality."
There are forty-eight pages of bibliography.

102. _____. Sexual Behavior in the Human Male. Philadelphia: Saunders, 1948.

This is the book that opened the door to serious homosexual research in the twentieth century. The relationship between religious background and the various sexual outlets, including homosexuality, is discussed on pages 465-487. There are twenty-two
pages of bibliography.

103. Kirk, Jerry. The Homosexual Crisis in the Mainline
Church: A Presbyterian Minister Speaks Out. Nashville, Tennessee: Nelson, 1978.

This strong statement against homosexuality was written by the pastor of the College Hill Presbyterian Church of Cincinnati to influence the General Assembly of that denomination in 1978. It did, as the Assembly refrained from giving a blanket approval of homosexual ordinations. Kirk does hold out, however, that there is hope for the homosexual in repentance.

104. Kopay, David, and Perry Deane Young. The David Kopay Story: An Extraordinary Self-Revelation. New York: Arbor House, 1977; rpt., New York: Bantam, 1977.

In December 1975 the ten-year veteran professional football player decided it was time to end his long personal nightmare and reveal his sexual preference for men--the first professional athlete ever to make such a revelation. He goes back and reveals the struggles of an entire lifetime--largely religious struggles in parochial schools and at a Catholic seminary. Highly personal.

105. Kosnik, Anthony, chairperson; William Carroll; Agnes Cunningham; Ronald Modras; and James Schulte. Human Sexuality: New Directions in American Catholic Thought. New York: Paulist, 1977; rpt., Garden City, New York: Doubleday, 1979.

This quite unofficial study--i.e., unofficial from the standpoint of the Roman Catholic hierarchy--of the Catholic Theological Society of America has been called "a watershed document." Pages 186-218 discuss "the homosexual" and homosexuality in general. The treatment views the homosexual condition favorably. The book is geared especially to pastoral needs.

106. LaHaye, Tim. The Unhappy Gays: What Everyone Should Know About Homosexuality. Wheaton, Illinois: Tyndale House, 1978.

LaHaye believes that there is a cure: "When Jesus Christ enters a person's life, he imparts to him a new set of desires and feelings." In the heart of the book he outlines an eighteen-point program for overcoming homosexuality. He then outlines a program for parents to follow when one of their children comes to them and announces, "I'm gay!"

107. Lauritsen, John, and David Thorstad. The Early Homosexual Rights Movement (1864-1935). New York: Times Change, 1974.

The earlier movement for homosexual liberation that is traced in this book began in the latter decades of the nineteenth century and ended with Hitler's concentration camps. There is some attention to Britain, but the movement was centered in Germany. This ninety-three-page paperback is a handy summary of names and events of importance during the period covered (note dates as integral part of the title).

108. Lewinsohn, Richard. A History of Sexual Customs. Trans. by Alexander Mayce. New York: Harper, 1958.

Contrary to what the title indicates, this book covers only the Western historical tradition. For a one-volume work, however, the treatment is noteworthy, especially those sections dealing with the ancient Greeks and with medieval Europe.

109. Licht, Hans [pseud. for Paul Brandt]. Sexual Life in Ancient Greece. Trans. by J. H. Freese. London: Routledge, 1932; rpt., New York: AMS, 1975.

This book is often seen in bibliographies dealing with sexuality, including homosexuality, in ancient Greece. It has been superseded now, however, by the work of K. J. Dover (see No. 45). Although Licht includes a great deal of information not found in Dover, according to some critics much of this may be misinformation.

110. Linehan, Kevin. Such Were Some of You. Scottdale, Pennsylvania: Herald, 1979.

After having a serious homosexual love affair that

did not work out, Linehan tried to escape from what he felt was inevitable heartbreak in homosexuality. He studied Greek, read Paul, and concluded that homosexuality was sinful. He says he changed, and others can too--hence the title, from Paul's Letter to the Romans.

111. Lovelace, Richard F. Homosexuality and the Church. Old Tappan, New Jersey: Revell, 1978.

This is a detailed presentation of the conservative point of view by an Evangelical theologian. Lovelace states that the theological and biblical arguments advanced to persuade the Church to change its traditional attitude toward the active homosexual lifestyle are not sufficiently persuasive.

112. Lucianus Samosatensis. The Syrian Goddess. Trans. by Herbert A. Strong and ed. by John Garstang. London: Constable, 1913.

It is difficult to overstate the importance of Lucian's The Syrian Goddess for the student of ancient religion. Among other things, it tells how devotees of the mother goddess carried out their act of self-castration (the description is on pages 84-85). This and other data illuminate the cult of the mother goddess, which was intimately associated with homosexuality in the Bible.

113. _____. The Syrian Goddess (De Dea Syria). Ed. by Harold W. Attridge and Robert A. Oden. Missoula, Montana: Scholars Press for the Society of Biblical Literature, 1976.

The Greek text is on one side of the page and the translation, largely prepared by Attridge, is on the other. Oden is responsible for the introduction. Note that the title page states: "Attributed to Lucian." On the importance of this work for biblical studies, see above, No. 112.

114. McNeill, John J. The Church and the Homosexual.

Mission, Kansas: Sheed, Andrews and McMeel, 1976; rpt., New York: Pocket Books, 1977.

This major work by a Jesuit theologian contends that the Bible does not condemn homosexuality as we understand it (inversion) but only perverse forms of it. His exegesis of Genesis 19 (Sodom story) and of Paul is largely gleaned from other scholars, namely D. S. Bailey and John Boswell; nevertheless, McNeill makes good use of psychological and practical arguments for the acceptance of "ethically responsible homosexual relationships."

115. Macourt, Malcolm, ed. Towards a Theology of Gay Liberation. London: SCM, 1977.

Macourt's 113-page paperback anthology contains essays on homosexuality and scripture and male homosexual relationships and lifestyles. The book does not cover lesbian relationships.

116. Marmor, Judd, ed. Homosexual Behavior: A Modern Reappraisal. New York: Basic Books, 1980.

A compendium of recent scholarship; various authors.

117. Martin, Del, and Phyllis Lyon. Lesbian/Woman. San Francisco: Glide, 1972; rpt., New York: Bantam, 1972.

This book, which discusses the whole spectrum of lesbian life and relationships, includes a dozen pages (pages 28-39 in the Bantam edition) on attitudes toward religion among homosexual women and the attitudes of the religions toward them. Included in the discussion are the biblical references to homosexuality.

117a. Mendola, Mary. The Mendola Report: A New Look at Gay Couples. New York: Crown, 1980.

Instead of looking only at their sexuality this book examines the entire lifestyles of approximately four hundred gay couples and finds that such relationships, conveniently called "marriages," are as stable as their heterosexual counterparts. Reviewer Jeannine Grammick notes that here is provided the kind of information on gay couples that church people need to reassess their positions on homosexuality.

118. Mickley, Richard R. Christian Sexuality: A Reflection on Being Christian and Sexual. 2d ed. with Study Guide. Los Angeles: Universal Fellowship, 1976.

A book designed to serve as a text for local church study courses on sexuality and homosexuality. It argues from the standpoint of the New Testament concept of love and is in the rather down-to-earth language of the Metropolitan Community Church, whose press issued it.

119. Milhaven, John G. Toward a New Catholic Morality. Garden City, New York: Doubleday, 1972.

120. Moore, Paul, Jr. Take a Bishop Like Me. San Francisco: Harper and Row, 1979.

An Episcopal bishop, who is himself heterosexual but who has agonized over the issue with some of his homosexual friends, including priests, takes a compassionate look at homosexuality. The ordination of the Reverend Ellen Barrett, first avowed lesbian priest, who was ordained by Bishop Moore in January 1977, is discussed and defended.

121. Morris, Paul. Shadow of Sodom. Wheaton, Illinois: Tyndale House, 1978.

122. Nelson, James B. Embodiment: An Approach to Sexuality and Christian Theology. Minneapolis: Augsburg, 1978.

The flesh does not oppose the spirit but embodies it, says Nelson, a United Church of Christ ethics professor. This book seeks to reconcile a traditional

Christian opposition to the body and, furthermore, to make a case for an affirmation of it. It contends that most forms of the sexual outlet, including homosexuality, are good and must be accepted. Notes and index.

123. Oberholzer, W. Dwight, ed. Is Gay Good? Ethics, Theology and Homosexuality. Philadelphia: Westminster, 1971.

A collection of essays both pro and con on the subject of homosexuality. The treatment is rather carefully balanced, but readers should keep in mind that the writers were addressing themselves to the points of view that prevailed at the beginning of the seventies rather than today.

124. Oraison, Marc. The Homosexual Question: An Attempt to Understand an Issue of Increasing Urgency Within a Christian Perspective. New York: Harper and Row, 1977.

The author, a French Catholic priest and psychiatrist, approaches the homosexual question as a counselor and therapist. He attempts to demonstrate the complexities and the involuntary nature of the homosexual orientation. He feels cases should be judged individually. Though at times Oraison tries to be neutral on the issue, his stance is quite liberal for a Roman Catholic priest.

125. Patai, Raphael. Sex and the Family in the Bible and the Middle East. Garden City, New York: Doubleday, 1959.

Patai is an anthropologist, folklorist, and biblical scholar. He relates the sexual data of the Old Testament to its context in the Middle East. Only pages 168-176 deal exclusively with homosexuality, but the topic is also discussed in connection with rape and sacred prostitution. He sees the David-Jonathan relationship as a love affair, as sexual, and as nothing unusual.

126. Perry, Troy, and Charles Lucas. The Lord Is My
     Shepherd and He Knows I'm Gay. Los Angeles:
     Nash, 1972; rpt., New York: Bantam, 1973.

     This is the autobiography of the Reverend Troy Per-
     ry, a former Pentecostal minister and founder of the
     Universal Fellowship of Metropolitan Community
     Churches, a homosexually orientated denomination.
     There are a number of pages devoted to the biblical
     references to homosexuality and how Perry responds
     to them.

127. Phillips, Anthony. Ancient Israel's Criminal Law: A
     New Approach to the Decalogue. New York: Schock-
     en, 1970.

     Phillips says that there is no condemnation of homo-
     sexuality in Israel's civil laws (the old Covenant Code
     of Exodus 20:22-23:33) and the Deuteronomic Code of
     Deuteronomy 12-26): the proscriptions appear for the
     first time in the later priestly (liturgical and cultic)
     laws of Leviticus. On this see pages 121-122.

128. Philpott, Kent. The Gay Theology. Plainfield, New
     Jersey: Logos International, 1977.

     Testimonies of homosexual persons who, according
     to this author, were able to change through "the pow-
     er of Christ." There is some discussion of the bib-
     lical material and suggestions for ministering to the
     special needs of "the homosexual."

128a. _____. The Third Sex? Plainfield, New Jersey:
     Logos International, 1975.

     Some testimonies of changed lives, biblical discus-
     sion concerning homosexuality, and guidelines for
     counseling homosexual persons "toward freedom in
     Christ."

129. Pintauro, Joseph. Cold Hands. New York: Simon
     and Schuster, 1979.

     This novel, by a former Roman Catholic priest,

discloses the slow coming-out process by a man whose homosexuality was long repressed. The setting moves from Brooklyn to Rome (where he studies for the priesthood) to Suffolk County, Long Island, New York.

130. Pittenger, W. Norman. Gay Lifestyles: A Christian Interpretation of Homosexuality and the Homosexual. Los Angeles: Universal Fellowship, 1977.

"For a homosexual it is natural, in my sense of the word, to wish to act, and to act, in a homosexual fashion, just as it is natural for a heterosexual to wish to act, and to act, in a heterosexual fashion." Pittenger speaks not for the Church but as a Christian and of the Church. The book is principally about males who are homosexual.

131. _____. Love and Control in Sexuality. Philadelphia: United Church, 1974.

This book has to do with heterosexual as well as homosexual orientation. By "control" Pittenger means that no one should treat another person as if he or she were only a "thing" or nothing more than a means to gratification. Relationships should be mutual and of such a kind that they promote growth for both partners.

132. _____. Making Sexuality Human. New York: United Church, 1970; 2d ed., 1979.

This is the renowned Anglican theologian's second book on sexuality and homosexuality (following Time for Consent; see No. 133). This one is a plea for acceptance of homosexuality and guidelines for loving relationships in general, whether homosexual or heterosexual. The major change in the two editions is in the Preface.

133. _____. Time for Consent. London: SCM, 1967.

This is Pittenger's detailed presentation of homosexu-

ality as an accepted part of the created order. It
is as much a part of that order as heterosexuality,
he says. This book was one of the first to be published in favor of homosexuality by a theologian of
outstanding repute. Note the date.

134. Ramm, Bernard L. The Right, the Good and the Hap-
py. Waco, Texas: Word Books, 1971.

This book is unusual coming from an Evangelical
teacher. It argues that homosexual practices were
a part of ancient religious rites and the biblical con-
demnations are addressed to this issue, or they are
in opposition to purely "sexual titillation." The main
problem, Ramm says, is with the negative attitude
toward it by the average Christian.

135. Rethford, William R. A Descriptive Field Research of
the Male Homosexual as a Requisite Toward a Strate-
gy of Christian Ministry. Doctoral dissertation,
Southern Baptist Theological Seminary, 1973.

136. Rinzema, J. The Sexual Revolution: Challenge and
Response. Grand Rapids, Michigan: Eerdmans,
1974.

Rinzema is concerned with the whole area of human
sexuality, with only a few pages devoted to homosexuality. He urges Christian moralists to "develop a
morality for homosexuality in consultation with homosexual people" and even goes so far as to call for
a "viable homosexual ethic," or a plea for the acceptance of permanent relationships in unchangeable
cases.

137. Robinson, Paul. The Modernization of Sex: Havelock
Ellis, Alfred Kinsey, William Masters and Virginia
Johnson. New York: Harper and Row, 1976.

Havelock Ellis, Alfred Kinsey, William Masters, and
Virginia Johnson are, after Freud, the most influential sexual thinkers of the century, according to Robinson, who discusses their contributions in depth.

Homosexuality is a topic throughout the book, and the Judeo-Christian sexual ethic is discussed on pages 76-77 and 82-86.

138. Rodgers, William D. The Gay Invasion: A Christian Look at the Spreading Homosexual Myth. Denver: Accent Books, 1977.

139. Rossman, Parker. Sexual Experience Between Men and Boys: Exploring the Pederast Underground. New York: Association, 1976.

Rossman discusses, with some empathy, the whole subject of pederasty both in ancient and modern times, with numerous examples from various cultures, most particularly from our own. There is some discussion of the New Testament references to homosexuality. Priests, counselors, and police officers are quoted. The book is especially geared to those who work with adolescent boys.

140. Sagarin, E. Odd Man In: Societies of Deviants in America. Chicago: Quadrangle, 1969.

Declares that the "contradictions in the homophile movement are likely to prevent it from becoming other than isolated and cultist, sinking deeper into untenable ideological distortion as it proclaims only that which its members want to hear and which they need (or feel they need) to believe."

141. Sanders, Dennis, ed. Gay Source: A Catalog for Men. New York: Berkley, 1977.

This is a general sourcebook on (male) homosexuality, telling where to find information about various aspects of the homosexual community. There are several pages on religion, featuring an article on the Universal Fellowship of the Metropolitan Community Churches, another on "Religious Caucuses and Organizations," and a third on "Books on Religion and Homosexuality."

142. Sarotte, George-Michael. Like a Brother, Like a
      Lover: Male Homosexuality in the American Novel
      and Theatre from Herman Melville to James Baldwin.
      Trans. by Richard Miller. Garden City, New York:
      Doubleday, 1978.

      The traditional Judeo-Christian ethic is discussed
      frequently in connection with leading writers in this
      survey of homosexual components in American litera-
      ture since 1850. Those treated in greatest detail
      are Melville, Jack London, Henry James, Ernest
      Hemingway, Scott Fitzgerald, William Inge, Truman
      Capote, Tennessee Williams, and Norman Mailer.
      Some elements discussed are misogyny, alcoholism,
      and masochism.

143. Scanzoni, Letha, and Virginia Ramey Mollenkott. Is
      the Homosexual My Neighbor? Another Christian
      View. San Francisco: Harper and Row, 1978.

      Two well-known Evangelical feminists team up to
      caution their fellow Christians against fear and hatred.
      They review briefly what the Bible and what science
      have to say, and ask, "Are Christians willing to be
      Christian?" Notes, annotated bibliography, and index.

144. Schmitt, Gladys. David the King. New York: Dial,
      1946; rpt., 1973.

      This fictional account of the life of David would prob-
      ably not raise many eyebrows today, but it was quite
      a jolt to many readers when it first appeared.
      David's love for both Jonathan and Bathsheba is de-
      picted, though neither equated nor compared. Each
      is seen as a particular phase of David's life at the
      time.

145. Schonauer, Bett, Brick Bradford, William P. Showalter,
      Leonard E. LeSourd, Catherine Jackson, and Robert
      C. Whitaker. Healing for the Homosexual. Oklaho-
      ma City: Presbyterian Charismatic Communion,
      1978.

      All six writers here state that homosexuality can and
      should be overcome.

146. Smedes, Lewis B. Sex for Christians: The Limits
and Liberties of Sexual Living. Grand Rapids,
Michigan: Eerdmans, 1976.

The relevant pages here are 62-73, but note that
they are a subdivision of a chapter entitled "Distorted
Sexuality." Smedes presents three options: (1) first,
try to change; (2) if that doesn't work, choose celibacy; and (3) if one cannot do that, then practice
"optimum homosexual morality" (a permanent relationship).

147. Smith, Morton. Clement of Alexandria and a Secret
Gospel of Mark. Cambridge, Massachusetts: Har-
vard University Press, 1973.

This is the technical work of philology that provides
the extensive background materials for the thesis
stated in Smith's The Secret Gospel (see No. 148).

148. _____. The Secret Gospel: The Discovery and
Interpretation of the Secret Gospel of Mark. New
York: Harper and Row, 1973.

Smith discloses a hitherto undiscovered second-
century text, the interpretation of which is that a
water baptism was administered by Jesus to chosen
disciples, who came to him singly and by night, clad
only in a linen cloth, and to whom he imparted the
mystery of the kingdom of God. The resultant freedom from the law of Moses may have been followed
by physical union. Speculative.

149. Sommers, Montague. The History of Witchcraft and
Demonology. New York: University Books, 1956.

Medieval views associated witchcraft, sodomy, and
heresy.

150. Steakley, James. The Homosexual Emancipation Movement in Germany. New York: Arno, 1975.

A clear and well-documented account of the origin

and growth of the German movement for homosexual
liberation--in fact, the best account.

151. Swicegood, Tom. Our God Too. New York: Pyramid,
1974.

This is the story of the founding of the Metropolitan
Community Church by Reverend Troy Perry and its
history up to the time this book was written. It includes some detailed discussion (on pages 143-159 and
225-228) of the biblical references to homosexuality
from the point of view of this homosexually orientated
denomination.

152. Symonds, John Addington. A Problem in Greek Ethics,
Being an Inquiry into the Phenomenon of Sexual Inversion. London: Privately printed, 1901. Numerous editions.

In turn-of-the-century England, following the Oscar
Wilde conviction, for scholars to look at the homo-
sexuality in the Greek classics was itself a trial.
But it's there, says Symonds, as for example in The
Symposium and Phaedrus, the two places where
Plato's teachings on love are to be found--and it is
love in a homosexual context.

153. _____. A Problem in Modern Ethics, Being an Inquiry into the Phenomenon of Sexual Inversion. London: Privately printed, 1891. Numerous editions.

This essay, long a classic in its field, very early
pointed up the conflict between a deep-rooted homosexual tradition in Western society and the modern
ethic that denied it. See also, by the same author,
A Problem in Greek Ethics (No. 152).

154. Szasz, Thomas. The Manufacture of Madness: A
Comparative Study of the Inquisition and the Mental
Health Movement. New York: Harper and Row,
1970.

The attempt of the modern psychiatric movement to

get people to become sexual conformists is compared
with the thinking of the Inquisition.   There is a
lengthy discussion of sodomy in connection with heresy in the Late Middle Ages.   Appendix ("A Synoptic
History of Persecutions for Witchcraft and Mental
Illness"), notes, and twenty pages of bibliography.

155.   Tannahill, Reay.   Sex in History.   Briarcliff Manor,
       New York: Stein and Day, 1980.

       Findings in such fields as anthropology, archaeology,
       biochemistry, physiology, and psychoanalysis illumi-
       nate sexual attitudes and practices in all the world's
       major civilizations from prehistoric times to the
       present.   Homosexuality is seen in context.

156.   Taylor, Gordon Rattray.   Sex in History.   London:
       Thames and Hudson, 1953; New York: Vanguard,
       1954; rpt., New York: Harper and Row, 1973.

       Taylor distinguishes two attitudes that have been
       dominant at one time or another in history: patrist
       periods, which possessed among other features, the
       notion that women were inferior to men, and matrist
       periods, in which women were accorded a high sta-
       tus.   It is only in the former, he says, that homo-
       sexuality has been regarded as an overwhelming dan-
       ger.   Much religious data is included in this one-
       volume history of human sexuality.

157.   Thielicke, Helmut.   The Ethics of Sex.   Trans. by
       John Doberstein.   New York: Harper and Row, 1964;
       rpt., Grand Rapids, Michigan: Baker, 1975.

       This important scholarly work regards homosexuality
       as a perversion in terms of a theological understand-
       ing of creation, but recognizes the dilemma of those
       who cannot achieve a reorientation to heterosexuality.
       It is best for them to be celibate, says Thielicke,
       but some ethically responsible relationships may be
       permitted.   The exegesis of Romans 1:26-27 is note-
       worthy.

158.   Twiss, Harold L., ed.   Homosexuality and the Chris-

tian Faith: A Symposium. Valley Forge, Pennsylvania: Judson, 1978.

A variety of views are presented here. "Homosex-
uality: An Overview," by Alan Bell, and "Some
Words of Caution," by William Muehl are reprinted
from Barnhouse and Holmes, Male and Female (see
No. 12). There is David Bartlett's essay from
Foundations (No. 186), and others by Letha Scanzoni,
Tracy Early, James Harrison, Lynn Buzzard, and
John Batteau. The points of view are balanced.

159. United Church of Christ. Human Sexuality: A Preliminary Study. New York: United Church, 1977.

The United Church Board for Homeland Ministries
was commissioned to conduct this 258-page study by
the 1975 General Synod of its denomination. It is
not always clear who wrote what here, but the principal writers appear to have been Ralph Weltge,
Phyllis Trible, Richard Scheef, and James Nelson.
There is a separate Study Guide for Human Sexuality
(fifty-seven pages) to accompany this text, which
looks favorably on the issue of homosexuality.

160. Valente, Michael. Sex: The Radical View of a Catholic Theologian. Milwaukee: Bruce, 1970.

161. Vanggaard, Thorkil. Phallos: A Symbol and Its History in the Male World. New York: International
Universities, 1974.

The penis as a symbol of power throughout history
is discussed, including phallic aggression, which this
author sees behind the Sodom story. The postexilic
Jewish purging of phallic elements within the cult led
to the suppression in Europe and America of what
Vanggaard calls the normal "homosexual radical" in
all men. Thorough documentation.

162. Warren, Patricia Nell. The Fancy Dancer. New York:
Morrow, 1976; rpt., New York: Bantam, 1977.

A gay novel about a Roman Catholic priest whose

confrontation with a young man in his parish forces
him to come to terms with his own sexuality. The
setting is a small town in Montana. Two elderly
lesbians appear as supporting characters.

163. Weeks, Jeffry. Coming Out: Homosexual Politics in
Britain, from the Nineteenth Century to the Present.
London: Quartet, 1977.

A clear and well-documented account of the origin
and growth of the homosexual-emancipation movement
in Great Britain. "Social purity" movements in late
Victorian England, says Weeks, led to the Labouchere
Amendment criminalizing homosexuality. Steps are
traced leading up to the decriminalization in 1967.

164. Weinberg, George. Society and the Healthy Homosexual. New York: St. Martin's, 1972; rpt., Garden
City, New York: Doubleday, 1973.

Freud, claims Weinberg, was more influenced by the
prevailing Judeo-Christian attitudes than he thought.
The religious background of "homophobia"--a word
coined by Weinberg here--is discussed from the beginning of the book through page 23 (paperback num-
bering). On "homophobia" see Geyer, No. 62.

165. Weinberg, Martin S., and Colin J. Williams. Male
Homosexuals: Their Problems and Adaptations. New
York: Oxford University Press, 1974.

The relevant chapters are 19: "Religious Background"
(pages 248-251) and 20: "Religiosity" (pages 252-
259). The authors find that those who interpret their
religion so as to understand it as not being violated
by their practice of homosexuality are the ones who
have the least problems in this area. There are
many Kinsey-type charts and scales.

166. Weltge, Ralph W., ed. The Same Sex: An Appraisal
of Homosexuality. Philadelphia: Pilgrim, 1969.

Eight of the essays in this book discuss homosexuality

rather neutrally, but three are from what was then the gradually awakening homophile movement. One of the latter is Barbara Gittings, who writes on "The Homosexual and the Church." From the former group Lewis E. Mattocks writes on "The Law and the Church vs. the Homosexual."

167. Westermarck, Edward. The Origin and Development of the Moral Ideas. 2 vols. 2d ed., London: Macmillan, 1917.

Vol. II of this magnum opus contains a hefty chapter on homosexuality that documents its existence in numerous societies. Most relevant here is the material from the Persian Vendidad, which Westermarck says was issued, like Leviticus, to keep its community "ritually pure." This is Westermarck's answer to the question of why homosexuality was stigmatized in the Judeo-Christian tradition.

168. White, Edmund. States of Desire: Travels in Gay America. New York: Dutton, 1980.

White's collection of essays on the contemporary homosexual scene examines "gay liberation," promiscuity, and the economic power of homosexuals and explores middle-class hedonism, drugs, violence, friendship, and religion in America. The discussion of homosexuality and Mormonism is noteworthy.

169. White, John. Eros Defiled. Downers Grove, Illinois: Inter-Varsity, 1977.

The author acknowledges that he himself was a reluctant homosexual participant in his youth. "Homosexuals, by and large," he says, "are unhappy people." Traditional approach.

170. Whitehead, Evelyn Easton, and James Whitehead. Christian Life Patterns: The Psychological Challenges and Religious Invitations of Adult Life. Garden City, New York: Doubleday, 1979.

Of particular interest here is the description of the

"coming out" process as a rite of adult passage that these authors relate to personal human growth and spiritual maturity for the homosexual. They also state that if the churches refuse to explore concretely and openly the challenges of the gay Christian life then they are also refusing to assist in the religious growth of their gay members.

171. Williams, Don. The Bond That Breaks: Will Homosexuality Split the Church? Los Angeles: BIM, 1978.

The author responds to the positions of several well-known writers who have defended homosexuality. He presents the gist of what some major theologians, such as Barth (see No. 13) and Thielicke (see No. 157), have said, and then draws his own anti-homosexual conclusions. He makes more use of Genesis 1-2 than do most authors.

172. Wolfenden Report. Report of the Committee on Homosexual Offenses and Prostitution (Great Britain). New York: Stein and Day, 1963.

This is the text of the report, largely instigated by the churches, that played a major role in the events leading up to the decriminalization of homosexuality in Britain.

173. Wood, Robert W. Christ and the Homosexual. New York: Vantage, 1960.

The significance of this book lies in its early date: Wood is one of the first writers who tried to tell the churches that they were going to have a problem with the issue of homosexuality. He is sympathetic, arguing from scripture and common sense; but no traditional publisher would touch his work in 1960. He had to pay to have his book published.

174. Woods, Richard. Another Kind of Love: Homosexuality and Spirituality. Chicago: Thomas More, 1977; rev. ed., Garden City, New York: Doubleday, 1978.

A Dominican priest takes note of the new attitude toward homosexual persons in today's society and makes recommendations for acceptance on all levels. The major stages in the life of the male homosexual are charted, with suggestions for ministry along the way. The Doubleday paperback gives more attention to lesbians than does the earlier hardback edition.

175. Wright, Ezekiel, and Daniel Inesse. God Is Gay: An Evolutionary Spiritual Work. San Francisco: Tayu, 1979.

Personal experiences growing out of one of the new spiritualities centered in the San Francisco area. The book bears a connection with the Tayu Institute, a predominately gay spiritual organization.

176. Young, Wayland. Eros Denied: Sex in Western Society. New York: Grove, 1964.

The history of Western attitudes toward all matters sexual is discussed in this one-volume survey.

II. ARTICLES AND ESSAYS

---

177. Abrams, J. Keith, et al. "Authoritarianism, Religiosity, and the Legalization of Victimless Crimes." Sociology and Social Research. Vol. 61, No. 1 (October 1977), pp. 68-82.

   An accidental sample of 161 students in introductory sociology answer a questionnaire. Slightly more than half (55 percent) indicated their support for the legalization of eight categories of victimless crimes, one of which was homosexuality. Two possible attitudinal correlates of support for legalization were also investigated: (1) authoritarianism, and (2) orthodox Christian belief, which revealed additional support data.

178. Abrook, M. F., et al. "Psychiatric Illness in the Clergy." British Journal of Psychiatry. Vol. 115, No. 521 (1969), pp. 457-463.

   Cases of psychiatric treatment of the clergy were compared with a previously reported sample of physicians. Clergy were older at the time of breakdown and had higher incidences of both organic psychoses and sexual deviations. Clergy live longer than physicians, and organic dementia may be more easily tolerated in parish work.

179. Adell, Arvid. "Process Thought and the Liberation

of Homosexuals." The Christian Century. Vol. 96, No. 2 (January 1979), pp. 46-48.

Process theology does not offer an easy answer to homosexuality, but it does provide a conception of God in which more positive affirmations can be made than in classical theology.

180. Aden, LeRoy. "Homosexuality: What Can the Church Say?" The Lutheran. Vol. 17, No. 9 (May 2, 1979), pp. 14-16.

Aden distinguishes between homosexual behavior and the homosexual condition. The Bible frowns on the former, he says. However, homosexually conditioned persons can only express their sexuality with others of the same sex and hence should not be condemned. It is not the use but the abuse of one's sexuality that is the sin.

181. Andersen, W. E., and B. V. Hill. "Homosexuality and the Education of Persons." Journal of Christian Education. Vol. 59 (September 1977), pp. 3-82.

Contents: Editorial--"Sexuality and Education," by W. E. Andersen and B. V. Hill; "Christians Take Another Look at Homosexuality," by Kenneth Orr; "Reflections on Homosexuality," by John Kleinig; and "Of Homosexuality: The Current State of Knowledge," by A. W. Steinbeck. Lengthy articles.

182. Apuzzo, Ginny, and Batya Bauman. "The Spectrum of Lesbian Experience: Religion," in Our Right to Love: A Lesbian Resource Book, ed. by Ginny Vida (Englewood Cliffs, New Jersey: Prentice-Hall, 1978), pp. 235-237.

Bauman says, "If there is any group of people who can claim more oppression than Jews, it is homosexuals." She writes of religion among lesbians from a particularly Jewish point of view, while Apuzzo speaks from a Roman Catholic background. "In high school the nuns would caution you against 'particular friendships,'" writes Apuzzo.

183. Aron, Harry. "The Homosexual." Journal of Human Relations. Vol. 17, No. 1 (1969), pp. 58-70.

Argues that homosexuality is "not a problem, not a danger, not an illness, not immaturity, not a taint, not a genetic demand, and the laws regarding homosexual behaviors are a fraud." Today's knowledge reveals that homosexual behavior cannot be unnatural (supported by a discussion of Freudian theory). "The so-called 'gay world' is, in almost all measures (interest, religiosity, liberalism, skills, etc. ... indistinguishable from the 'non-gay world.'" Claims for normality are moralisms disguised as a science.

184. Barnhouse, Ruth Tiffany. "Response to My Critics." Anglican Theological Review. Vol. 59 (April 1977), pp. 194-197.

Response to the Hydes and others (see Nos. 11 and 286).

185. Barrett, Ellen M. "Gay People and Moral Theology," in The Gay Academic, ed. by Louie Crew (Palm Springs, California: ETC, 1978), pp. 329-333.

This is a scholarly Christian homosexual apologetic. Of interest is the author's fear that when gay males are accepted (because their sexuality affirms the virtues of maleness) and heterosexual women (because they relate closely to men) lesbians will still be out in the cold "because our sexuality is a total and radical affirmation of woman-nature, which the Church has never allowed."

186. Bartlett, David L. "A Biblical Perspective on Homosexuality." Foundations: Baptist Journal of History and Theology. Vol. 20, No. 2 (April-June 1977), pp. 133-147.

This article finds the biblical references to homosexuality unequivocally to be condemnatory, although Romans 1:26-27 is seen primarily as a condemnation of idolatry. God's grace, however, is stronger than any condemnation; hence Bartlett argues ultimately in favor of acceptance.

187. Barton, G. A. "Sodomy." Encyclopedia of Religion and Ethics, ed. by James Hastings. Vol. II (1928), pp. 672-674.

Discusses sodomy among the ancient Hebrews, in Babylonia, in India, and among the aborigines of Australia. Barton attests that among the Hebrews sodomy was practiced by men consecrated to a deity and consummated within a temple in the service of religion (up to the time of King Josiah).

188. Bauer, Paul F. "Homosexual Subculture at Worship: A Participant Observation Study." Pastoral Psychology. Vol. 25 (Winter 1976), pp. 115-127.

189. Baum, Gregory. "Catholic Homosexuals." Commonweal. Vol. 99, No. 19 (February 15, 1974), pp. 479-482.

Baum states that Dignity, the international Catholic homosexual organization, presents a challenge to Catholic theology. The old arguments against homosexuality based on human nature will have to be re-examined, he says, although he does not visualize Catholicism changing its stance in the near future. Meanwhile Dignity should maintain a strong minority position within the Church.

190. Bieber, Irving. "A Discussion of 'Homosexuality: The Ethical Challenge.'" Journal of Consulting and Clinical Psychology. Vol. 44, No. 2 (April 1976), pp. 163-166.

191. Birchard, Roy. "Metropolitan Community Church: Its Development and Significance." Foundations: Baptist Journal of History and Theology. Vol. 20, No. 2 (April-June 1977), pp. 127-132.

This is a brief history of the predominately gay church, from its beginnings down to 1977. Birchard points out that the new denomination would not exist had there not been a need for it.

192. Bowman, Frank Paul. "The Religious Metaphors of a Married Homosexual: Marcel Jouhandeau's Chronique d'une passion," in Homosexualities and French Literature, ed. by George Stambolian and Elaine Marks (Ithaca, New York: Cornell University Press, 1979), pp. 295-311.

This critical analysis of the contemporary French writer's 1964 novel focuses on his extensive and somewhat contradictory use of religious, especially Catholic, metaphor to delineate homosexual love and heterosexual love, good and evil, the religious and the sacrilegious.

193. Boyd, Kenneth M. "Homosexuality and the Church," in Understanding Homosexuality: Its Biological and Psychological Bases, ed. by J. A. Loraine (New York: American Elsevier, 1974), pp. 165-186.

194. Boyd, Malcolm, and Edward J. Curtin. "Mask-Wearing: Spiritually Stifling." Christian Century. Vol. 96, No. 3 (January 24, 1979), pp. 79-81.

Two responses to William H. Willimon's "Reader's Response" in regard to Boyd's book Take Off the Masks (see No. 21), in an earlier issue of Christian Century (November 8, 1978). Critical of Willimon for bringing up the sexuality of Jesus, Boyd says that this "can become a convenient distraction from the subject of Jesus' treatment of others." Curtin supports Boyd.

195. Boyd, Malcolm, and Virginia Ramey Mollenkott. "Homosexual Love: An Explanation/An Exploration." Insight: A Quarterly of Lesbian/Gay Christian Opinion. Vol. 3, No. 4 (Fall 1979), pp. 5-8.

Mollenkott attempts to show how homosexual relationships are not much different from heterosexual ones as far as everyday human problems are concerned. And many of these relationships still succeed, though church and society have traditionally put stumbling blocks in their way. Boyd's contribution is five prayers using poetic imagery and example from life to illustrate homosexual relationships.

196. Boyfrank, Monwell [pseud.]. "Lot, Sodom, Onan and Paul." ONE Magazine. Vol. 16, No. 4 (July-August 1972), pp. 10-15.

197. Bratten, Honorius. "Can a Homosexual Be Christian?" ONE Magazine. Vol. 12, No. 8 (August 1964), pp. 7-12.

198. Brick, Barrett L. "Judaism in the Gay Community," in Positively Gay, ed. by Betty Berzon and Robert Leighton (Millbrae, California: Celestial Arts, 1979), pp. 79-87.

Judaism by its very nature cannot grant legitimacy to discrimination. These are societal attitudes, not religious ones. The addresses of a number of gay synagogues are listed and the growth of the gay Jewish movement is detailed.

199. Browning, Don S. "Homosexuality, Theology, the Social Sciences, and the Church." Encounter. Vol. 40, No. 3 (Summer 1979), pp. 223-243.

Browning evaluates three recent denominational studies that address the question of homosexuality: the Disciples of Christ's "Study Document on Homosexuality and the Church"; the United Church of Christ study, Human Sexuality: A Preliminary Study; and, finally, Roman Catholic positions, principally Human Sexuality, a cooperative venture by the Catholic Theological Society of America.

200. Bryant, Florence. "The Church and the Homosexual." Trends (July-August 1973), pp. 10-18.

This article from a now-defunct Presbyterian publication explores the whole subject of homosexuality from the standpoint of those who know little or nothing about it, tries to answer their questions, and then asks questions of them in regard to their attitudes toward homosexual persons. Geared for discussion groups.

201. Burton, Richard. "Terminal Essay, The Book of the Thousand Nights and a Night: Pederasty," in Homosexuality: A Cross Cultural Approach, ed. by Donald Webster Cory (New York: Julian, 1956), pp. 207-247.

This essay, which was appended to Burton's famed translation of Arabian Nights (1886), describes homosexual practices among numerous peoples, mainly Muslim and other non-Christian peoples that Burton knew at first hand. It concludes that the suppression of homosexuality is only found in nations that have stemmed from a Judeo-Christian background.

202. Cahill, Lisa Sowle. "Sexual Issues in Christian Theological Ethics: A Review of Recent Studies." Religious Studies Review. Vol. 4, No. 1 (January 1978), pp. 1-14.

Cahill presents an overview of most of the important works dealing with sexuality, including homosexuality, that have appeared during the past several years. Her judgment is quite critical: she finds all of the works lacking in one area or another. There is an important bibliography attached.

203. Campion, Michael A., and Alfred A. Barrow. "When Was the Last Time You Hugged a Homosexual?" Journal of the American Scientific Affiliation. Vol. 29, No. 3 (1977), pp. 10-11.

Interpreted, the title means, "When was the last time I reached out beyond myself and cared for and tried to understand the homosexual?" States that there is a continuum, or degrees, of homosexuality. Replies by several authors.

204. Campolo, Anthony. "A Christian Sociologist Looks at Homosexuality." The Wittenburg Door. No. 39 (October-November 1977), pp. 16-17.

Campolo writes that there are causes for homosexual behavior, some biological, some sociological, other than those that Paul condemned. "These latter types of homosexuals are not perverting their original nature." Though Campolo says he disapproves of homosexual behavior (to be distinguished from a homosexual orientation) he can see no valid reason for discrimination where civil rights are concerned.

205. Carrier, J. M. "Cultural Factors Affecting Urban, Mexican Male Homosexual Behavior." Archives of Sexual Behavior. Vol. 5, No. 3 (May 1976), pp. 211-222.

206. Carson, Steve. "Please, No Spectators." Christianity and Crisis. Vol. 39, No. 10 (June 11, 1979), pp. 157-159.

This article is in the form of a classroom presentation on "gay liberation" that took place in a course on "Liberation Theology for North Americans" at Union Theological Seminary on April 24, 1979. The author was a second-year student there at the time. Poetic readings aim at highlighting the anguish of homosexual men and women, including those who were then students at the seminary.

207. Cartwright, John H. "Homosexuality: A Behavioral Science/Cross Cultural Approach." Explor. Vol. 1, No. 2 (Fall 1975), pp. 52-61.

208. Chafetz, Janet F., et al. "A Study of Homosexual Women." Social Work. Vol. 19, No. 6 (November 1974), pp. 714-723.

Says that there is a paucity of research concerning homosexual women, and much that there is reflects prejudice against both women and homosexuals. Thus the type of information available to those in the helping professions is totally inadequate. Data on religious institutions and homosexual women in Houston, Texas, are a part of one recent study that is included here.

209. Clark, Joan L. "Coming Out: The Process and Its

Price." Christianity and Crisis. Vol. 39, No. 10
(June 11, 1979), pp. 149-153.

A staff member of the Women's Division, Board of
Global Ministries, United Methodist Church, outlines
step by step the process whereby her employment
with the Methodist board was terminated following the
announcement of her lesbianism within the context of
one of her own board reports. See also editorial "In
the Matter of Joan L. Clark" in the same issue (No.
287).

210. Clarkson, Margaret. "Singleness: His Share for Me."
Christianity Today. Vol. 23, No. 10 (February 16,
1979), pp. 510-511.

Singleness, homosexuality, and a few other things
were not a part of God's original plan. Hence the
church should take a long, compassionate look not
only at the needs of its homosexuals but of all its
singles. There is no other group in the Christian
family, Clarkson says, for whom so little ministry
is provided.

211. Clemons, James T. "Toward a Christian Affirmation
of Human Sexuality." Religion in Life. Vol. 43,
No. 4 (Winter 1974), pp. 425-435.

212. Coleman, Gerald D. Homosexuality--An Appraisal.
Chicago: Franciscan Herald, 1978.

In this eighty-nine-page monograph Coleman does
some fence-walking on the issue. He seems to want
to be accepting--and is, where civil rights are
concerned--but ultimately he takes his stand with the
December 29, 1975, "Declaration on Certain Questions
Concerning Sexual Ethics" and the November 11, 1976,
document of the American Catholic bishops entitled
"To Live in Christ Jesus." Footnotes--and an Im-
primatur.

213. "A Colloquy on Homosexuality and the Church." The
Circuit Rider. Vol. 4, No. 3 (March 1980), pp. 3-
13.

Six articles in the United Methodist clergy magazine.

214. Court, John H. "Homosexuality: A Scientific and Christian Perspective." Interchange. No. 13 (1973), pp. 22-40.

Reviews homosexuality from scientific, moral, religious, and legal perspectives. Discusses causation and suggested treatments. A Christian moral background is offered, and the (Australian) legal position is delineated.

215. _____, and Raymond Johnston. "Psychosexuality: A Three-Dimensional Model." Journal of Pastoral Theology. Vol. 6, No. 2 (1978), pp. 90-97.

Proposes a three-dimensional model to represent the continuum of homosexuality-heterosexuality, of orientation and activity, and of morality--that is, a spiritual dimension that is overlooked by secular and humanistic researchers. It examines a specific case of homosexuality in the light of this model.

216. Cowan, Wayne H., et al. "The Debate on Homosexuality: We Vote for Change." Christianity and Crisis. Vol. 37, Nos. 9-10 (May 30-June 13, 1977), pp. 114-116 (combined issue).

In this three-page editorial article the editors of C&C say that the untouchable issue is now unavoidable, though no one is obliged to move farther than his or her conscience will allow. But the burden of proof, they say, rests on those who would "maintain the policy of oppression."

217. _____. "Defining the Issue in San Diego: Gay Questions, Straight Answers." Christianity and Crisis. Vol. 38, No. 6 (May 1, 1978), pp. 98-100.

This is an editorial in the form of an article addressed to the United Presbyterian General Assembly of 1978. A study commission of the denomination had prepared a majority report recommending that avowed homosexual candidates for the ministry might under certain conditions be ordained. The editorial urges the forthcoming convention to accept the report.

218. Craddock, Fred. "How Does the New Testament Deal with the Issue of Homosexuality?" Encounter. Vol. 40, No. 3 (Summer 1979), pp. 197-208.

Professor Craddock addresses himself to the ways in which the early Church dealt or did not deal with homosexuality on the basis of what evidence there is. He expands on the New Testament usage of "lists" (as I Corinthians 6:9-10 and I Timothy 1:9-10) and advises caution. Unless we use material the way the New Testament itself uses it, he says, we cannot lay claim to "being scriptural."

219. Crew, Louie. "At St. Luke's Parish: The Peace of Christ Is Not for Gays." Christianity and Crisis. Vol. 37, Nos. 9-10 (May 30-June 13, 1977), pp. 140-144 (combined issue).

A professor of English at a Southern state college delineates the oppression he has felt from a small community where he lived openly with a lover of the same sex. He tells how he was only reluctantly served Holy Communion at the local Episcopal parish where he chose to worship.

220. _____. "The Church and the Gays." Christianity and Crisis. Vol. 40, No. 1 (February 4, 1980), pp. 2, 14.

Crew charges here that heterosexuals are trying to maintain the Church as a private club. The real test, he says, is whether the Church will behave toward gays as children of God.

221. _____. "Concerning Love and Charity." The Witness. Vol. 59, No. 2 (February 1976), p. 11.

A rejoinder to Brian McNaught's "Dilemma of the Gay

in the Church" in the same issue. McNaught is perhaps the leading Catholic gay journalist, Crew the
founder of Integrity, national society for gay Episcopalians and their friends.

222. _____. "Homosexuality: An Integrity Leader's
View." The Living Church. Vol. 173, No. 5 (August 1, 1976), pp. 8, 11-12.

223. _____. "Just as I Am: Louie Crew's Account of
Growing Up Gay in Dixie." Southern Exposure. Vol.
5, No. 1 (Summer 1977), pp. 59-63.

224. _____. "The New Leaven in the Loaf." Metanoia.
Vol. 8, No. 3 (September 1976), pp. 2-3.

225. _____. "One Fold and One Shepherd." The Church-
man. Vol. 188, No. 5 (June-July 1974), p. 15.

226. _____. "Walking with Dignity." Insight: Quarterly
of Gay Catholic Opinion. First Anniversary Issue.
Vol. 2, No. 1 (Autumn 1977), pp. 20-21.

227. Crompton, J. "Jeremy Bentham's Essay on Pederasty." Journal of Homosexuality. Vol. 3, No. 4
(Summer 1978), pp. 383-387.

228. Crompton, Louis. "Gay Genocide: From Leviticus to
Hitler," in The Gay Academic, ed. by Louie Crew
(Palm Springs, California: ETC, 1978), pp. 67-91.

A long essay, citing cases of homosexual persecution,
including executions, from A.D. 342 until the time
of Hitler. Leviticus 20:18 is frequently cited as the
justification for the executions--hence the article's
title. There are critical notes and an appendix con-
taining some primary documents relating to the Dutch
persecution of 1730-31.

229. Cruikshank, Margaret. "Is This the Reward of a Cath-

olic Girlhood?, " in The Coming Out Stories, ed. by
Julia Penelope and Susan J. Wolfe (Watertown, Massachusetts: Persephone, 1980), pp. 31-35.

The conservative background of parochial-school
training accompanies this homosexual woman long into
adulthood: it was, however, a factor that was to be
overcome in her painful coming-out process. Religious references in the forty other stories contained
in this same volume are sparse.

230. Curran, Charles E. "Homosexuality, " in "Sexuality
and Sin: A Current Reappraisal. " Homoletic and
Pastoral Review. Vol. 69, No. 1 (October 1968),
p. 31.

231. _____. "Homosexuality and Moral Theology: Meth-
odological and Substantive Considerations. " The
Thomist. Vol. 35, No. 3 (July 1971), pp. 447-484.

232. Davidson, G. C. "Homosexuality: The Ethical Challenge. " Journal of Consulting and Clinical Psychology. Vol. 44, No. 2 (April 1976), pp. 157-162.

See responses to this article under Bieber (No. 190)
and Halleck (No. 264).

233. Devor, Richard C. "Homosexuality and St. Paul. "
Pastoral Psychology. Vol. 23, No. 224 (May 1972),
pp. 50-58.

Argues that Paul's list in I Corinthians 6:9-10 reflects the Jewish view of the Gentile world as popu-
lated by those guilty of assorted perversions. But
grace is for everyone and no sin precludes its opera-
tion. Paul is saying that conversion ought to change
habits, but his writings indicate that this conversion
did not bring total, immediate change. If it did,
many of his exhortations would have been pointless.

234. Dlugos, Tim. "A Cruel God: The Gay Challenge to
the Catholic Church. " Christopher Street. Vol. 4,
No. 9 (September 1979), pp. 20-39.

This article by a freelance writer is an insider's look at the homosexuality within the Roman Catholic Church, revealing among other things how casual homosexual affairs are often tolerated while love affairs with commitment are forbidden. Dlugos interviewed several priests and sisters who are working openly with homosexual Catholics and also reports on the active Dignity Chapter of New York.

235. Dostourian, Ara. "Gayness: A Radical Christian Approach," in The Gay Academic, ed. by Louie Crew (Palm Springs, California: ETC, 1978), pp. 335-349.

Dostourian claims that Christianity's idea of affirming heterosexual marriage as the only valid form of the sexual outlet is not constant with the sexual picture of the twentieth century—in fact it never has been. He says that "the Church must take a very open attitude to various sexual orientations and various forms of human relationships ... as long as these are conducted in a loving and responsible way."

236. Doughty, Darrell J. "Homosexuality and Obedience to the Gospel." Church and Society. Vol. 67, No. 5 (May-June 1977), pp. 12-23.

Doughty argues that we cannot appeal to New Testament rules to be justified, for this itself would be contrary to New Testament teaching. He reviews the meaning of kata phusin ("in accordance with nature") and other concepts that related to homosexuality in New Testament times and finds no historical solutions to personal questions. The answer, he says, must be theological, and the New Testament itself supplies it.

237. Driver, Tom. "Homosexuality: The Contemporary and Christian Contexts. Commonweal. Vol. 98, No. 5 (April 6, 1973), pp. 103-106.

There is an elaboration of this discussion in the June 1, 1973, issue of the same periodical.

238. _____. "Sexuality and Jesus." Union Seminary

Quarterly Review. Vol. 20, No. 3 (March 1965), pp. 235-246.

The lack of evidence in the Gospels in regard to the sexuality of Jesus may be deliberate. In the other religions, puritanical or orgiastic, sex was made a principal concern--but not here. Reprinted in Sex: Thoughts for Contemporary Christians, ed. by Michael J. Taylor (Doubleday, 1972).

239. Duque, Asterio. "Homosexuality: A Theological Evaluation." The Priest (March 1975), pp. 30-37; (April 1975), pp. 19-25; and (May 1975), pp. 26-31.

240. Early, Tracy. "The Struggle in the Denominations: Shall Gays Be Ordained?" Christianity and Crisis. Vol. 37, Nos. 9-10 (May 30-June 13, 1977), pp. 118-122 (combined issue).

Early surveys how the mainline churches--United Church of Christ, Methodists, Presbyterians (UPC and PCUS), Episcopalians, Baptists, and Lutherans-- have approached this issue since 1972. There is also some mention of the Eastern Orthodox bodies and the Synagogue Council of America and their approaches. The attitude of some of the seminaries toward their openly homosexual students is also discussed.

241. Enroth, R. M. "Homosexual Church: An Ecclesiastical Extension of a Sub-Culture." Social Compass. Vol. 21, No. 3 (1974), pp. 355-360.

This author later collaborated with Gerald E. Johnson on a book on this same subject--The Gay Church (No. 49).

242. Espy, John W., and James B. Nelson. "Continuing the Discussion: 'Homosexuality and the Church.'" Christianity and Crisis. Vol. 37, Nos. 9-10 (May 30-June 13, 1977), pp. 116-118 (combined issue).

This article was provoked by Professor Nelson's pro-homosexual article in the previous issue of C&C

(see No. 336). Espy, a senior seminarian, argues that homosexuality is condemned by scripture and works against wholeness in persons. Nelson replies.

243. Evans, Ted. D. "Homosexuality: Christian Ethics and Psychological Research." Journal of Psychology and Theology. Vol. 3 No. 2 (Spring 1975), pp. 94-98.

A proposal for a Christian ethic on homosexuality, with relevant biblical passages and psychological studies cited. Distinction is made between homosexual condition and behavior. While those representing the former, being blameless for their condition, ought to be embraced by the Church, the practicing homosexual is not to be seen as blameless and ought to be drawn gradually to "God's created ideal."

244. Eyrich, Howard A. "Hope for the Homosexual: The Case for Nouthetic Help." Journal of Pastoral Practice. Vol. I, No. 2 (Summer 1977), pp. 19-33.

After presenting his position that homosexuality is not of genetic origin, Eyrich gives his arguments for its being a learned behavior. He further insists that through sympathetic and understanding counseling the behavior can be overcome. His program of relearning he calls "nouthetic counseling," the main steps of which are outlined in the remainder of the article.

245. Fehren, Henry. "A Christian Response to Homosexuals." U.S. Catholic (September 1972), pp. 6-11.

246. Fink, Peter. "Homosexuality: A Pastoral Hypothesis." Commonweal. Vol. 100, No. 8 (April 6, 1973), pp. 107-112.

247. Fisher, David H. "The Homosexual Debate: A Critique of Some Critics." St. Luke's Journal of Theology. Vol. 22, No. 3 (June 1979), pp. 176-184.

This article is double-pronged: on the one hand it discusses the rightness or wrongness of homosexuality from a philosophical point of view and comes to no conclusion; on the other hand it asks what the Church should do about it. For an answer to the latter question it suggests what it calls a "classical Anglican compromise," which is: Do nothing at the present time.

248. Floerke, Jill Drum. "Ministering to Gay Christians." The Christian Century. Vol. 93, No. 32 (October 13, 1976), pp. 854-856.

The title of this article is somewhat misleading in that it is not an essay on pastoral care: it is an overview of John McNeill's The Church and the Homosexual (No. 114) from this author's perspective.

249. Flynn, Charles P. "Sexuality and Insult Behavior." Journal of Sex Behavior. Vol. 12, No. 1 (February 1976), pp. 1-13.

Although completely absent in primitive societies, insults based on references to homosexual behavior are numerous in advanced cultures, particularly in the United States. In some societies sex-related insults are related functionally to the maintenance of religious beliefs and values. It is suggested that insults indicate the boundaries of acceptable sexual behavior in a given culture.

249a. Franklin, Patrick. "Religion: Bond or Bondage for Gays." The Advocate. No. 306 (1980), pp. 21-23.

The brunt of this article is: Why should gay people ally themselves with any group within the Judeo-Christian tradition that, if it knew of their sexual orientation, would shun them? Yet, he says, many do. He argues against their doing so and against Christianity in particular on the basis of its past record.

250. Fuliga, Hose B. "Christian Moral Theological Reflection on the Ethical Issue of Homosexuality." South East Asia Journal of Theology. Vol. 16, No. 2 (1975), pp. 40-44.

251. Furnish, Dorothy Jean. "The Treatment of Sexuality in Church School Curriculum Materials." Explor. Vol. 1, No. 2 (Fall 1975), pp. 62-70.

252. Gay, Calvin [pseud.]. "To the Presbyterians on Homosexuality: You Spoke from Ignorance." Christianity and Crisis. Vol. 38, No. 16 (October 30, 1978), pp. 254-259.

   This minister, writing anonymously to the United Presbyterian General Assembly, says that the Assembly's 1978 policy statement that homosexual pastors must lead celibate lives was itself sinful in "telling them that the price of their full acceptance by their church is to agree to lead barren and lonely lives." He also criticizes what he considers the arbitrary use of the Bible in the statement.

253. Gearhart, Sally. "Lesbianism and God-the-Father." Radical Religion. Vol. 1, No. 1 (Spring 1974), pp. 19-21.

   Reprinted in Body Politic, Vol. 16 (December 1974), pp. 12-13, 23; and in other publications.

254. Gerard, Robert. "Daddy's Boys." Christopher Street. Vol. 4, No. 9 (September 1979), pp. 43-57.

   This article is really an excerpt from a forthcoming book that, when published, will be the first gay novel ever written by a functioning Roman Catholic priest, at least as far as we know. The author is a Jesuit: he describes a Jesuit seminary professor and his coterie of favorites, who are known as "Daddy's Boys." Homosexuality is openly implied in many behind-the-scene situations but never publicly acknowledged, since officially it does not exist.

255. Glaser, Chris. "A Newly Revealed Christian Experience." Church and Society. Vol. 67, No. 5 (May-June 1977), pp. 5-11.

   This article is in the form of a personal confessional

of the author, who explains why he feels compelled
to be both homosexual and Christian. Yet, he says,
for most persons "coming out" is something they can
do only outside the Church. But for those who want
to stay in Christian community "the church has meant
more than just a closet ... the church has become
for them a giant tomb."

256. Goodich, Michael. "Sodomy in Ecclesiastical Law and
Theory." Journal of Homosexuality. Vol. 1, No. 4
(Summer 1976), pp. 427-434.

The author later incorporated the substance of this
article, and of the article listed immediately below
(No. 257), into his book The Unmentionable Vice
(No. 65).

257. _____. "Sodomy in Medieval Secular Law." Journal of Homosexuality. Vol. 1, No. 3 (Spring 1976),
pp. 295-302.

258. Gordon, Sol. "It's Not Okay to Be Anti-Gay." The
Witness. Vol. 60, No. 10 (October 1977), pp. 10-
13, 16.

Gordon comments on the biblical references to homosexuality, dismisses "latent homosexuality," and
points out that "to come out" is a political statement.
He relates the homosexual-rights movement to the
women's movement and discusses both with a great
deal of wit to accompany his defense of them.

259. Greenberg, Jerrold. "A Study of Male Homosexuals
(Predominately College Students)." Journal of the
American College Health Association. Vol. 22, No.
1 (October 1973), pp. 56-60.

A questionnaire was administered to eighty-six homosexual males--fifty-three of them college students,
all belonging to homophile organizations--concerning
sexual behavior, family background, religious attitudes, etc. Religion was found to be of little importance in these students' lives. Most had no prefer-

ence for one particular sexual behavior, whether fellatio or anal intercourse, active or passive role. Sixty percent had experienced heterosexual intercourse.

260. Griffin, David R. "Ordination for Homosexuals? Yes." Encounter. Vol. 40, No. 3 (Summer 1979), pp. 265-272.

261. Gross, Alfred A. "Thesis, Antithesis, Synthesis." Pastoral Psychology. Vol. 22, No. 219 (December 1971), pp. 41-44.

Homosexuals are human beings, and, despite their behavior in this regard, to treat them as otherwise abnormal is inhumane and pragmatically unrealistic.

262. Haas, Harold L. "Homosexuality." Currents in Theology and Mission. Vol. 5, No. 2 (April 1978), pp. 82-104.

This long and comprehensive essay summarizes the principal evidence in regard to homosexuality--the biblical, sociological, and psychiatric--and reveals the respect that this Lutheran author has for a scholarly approach to the issue. His conclusion is that the churches should be accepting of ethically structured one-on-one homosexual relationships.

263. Haeberle, Erwin J. "Historical Roots of Sexual Oppression," in The Sexually Oppressed, ed. by Harvey L. and Jean S. Gochros (New York: Association, 1977), pp. 3-27.

See newer work by the same author, above (No. 74).

264. Halleck, S. L. "Another Response to 'Homosexuality: The Ethical Challenge.'" Journal of Consulting and Clinical Psychology. Vol. 44, No. 2 (April 1976), pp. 167-170.

264a. Halloran, Joe. Understanding Homosexual Persons. Hicksville, New York: Exposition, 1979.

The author, a Roman Catholic priest, spent a sabbatical year in the San Francisco Bay area and became involved with a local Dignity chapter. In this book he defends this involvement and states a case for the role of gay people in the church. A question-and-answer format is employed. The work appears to be addressed primarily to a heterosexual audience.

265. Harrison, James. "The Dynamics of Sexual Anxiety." Christianity and Crisis. Vol. 37, Nos. 9-10 (May 30-June 13, 1977), pp. 136-140 (combined issue).

Harrison deals with the anxieties about homosexuality that are a part of our Judeo-Christian cultural heritage, the fear of raising children without a heterosexual model, the fear of homosexuality in some males as an extension of their hostility toward women. It is this fear of homosexuality that is destructive, he says, rather than homosexuality per se.

266. Harvey, John F. "Homosexuality." The New Catholic Encyclopedia. Vol. 7 (1967), pp. 116-119.

After an introduction, section headings are Classification, Incidence of Homosexuality, Society and the Homosexual, Morality of Homosexuality, and Pastoral Guidance (a sample of which is: "Pastoral experience reveals that the priest can inspire the invert to undertake apostolic work for the Church as a means of spiritual adjustment and fulfillment"). Bibliography.

267. _____. "Reflections on a Retreat for Clerics with Homosexual Tendencies." Linacre Quarterly. Vol. 46, No. 13 (May 1979), pp. 6-40.

Reflects the traditional Catholic viewpoint. There are thirteen additional articles by Harvey, dating between 1955 and 1974, listed in Vern L. Bullough et al., An Annotated Bibliography of Homosexuality (No. 450).

268. Hay, Henry. "The Moral Climate of Canaan at the Time of the Judges." ONE Institute Quarterly. No.

1 (Spring 1958), pp. 8-16; and No. 2 (Summer 1958), pp. 50-59.

269. Haynes, Stephen N., and L. Jerome Oziel. "Homo-sexuality: Behaviors and Attitudes." Archives of Sexual Behavior. Vol. 5, No. 4 (July 1976), pp. 283-289.

Results of a questionnaire submitted to 4,251 under-graduate students indicate that homosexual experience was significantly lower than what is commonly re-ported in the literature, and not related to race, re-ligion, or residence. Amazingly, students reporting homosexual experience did not express a lower rate of heterosexual activity coinciding with homosexual experience.

270. Hencken, Joel D. "Homosexuals and Heterosexuals: We Are All Apologists." Anglican Theological Re-view. Vol. 59 (April 1977), pp. 191-193.

271. Henley, Nancy M., and Fred Pincus. "Interrelation-ship of Sexist, Racist, and Anti-Homosexual Atti-tudes." Pyschological Reports. Vol. 42, No. 1 (February 1978), pp. 83-90.

Some 211 undergraduates responded to a seven-point questionnaire with subscales on racial, sexual, and homosexual groups. Data on political orientation, religious affiliation and involvement, and parents' educational level were also obtained. All three forms of prejudice were higher for those professing more religious involvement, with more bias found at the conservative end of the spectrum.

272. Henry, George W. "Pastoral Counseling for Homo-sexuals," in Homosexuality: A Cross Cultural Ap-proach, ed. by Donald Webster Cory (New York: Julian, 1956), pp. 384-393.

The minister, states Dr. Henry, must seek to re-store self-respect in homosexual individuals, bring them into a working relationship with themselves, and help them to face the world with optimism. This essay first appeared, significantly, five years earlier, in Pastoral Psychology (November 1951).

273. Henry, Patrick. "Homosexuals: Identity and Dignity." Theology Today. Vol. 33 (April 1976), pp. 33-39.

274. Hessert, Paul. "Toward a Theology of Sexuality." Explor. Vol. 1, No. 2 (Fall 1975), pp. 78-87.

"Not the structures of procreation but those of communion define the human function of sexuality," concludes Hessert.

275. Heyward, Carter. "Coming Out: Journey Without Maps." Christianity and Crisis. Vol. 39, No. 10 (June 11, 1979), pp. 153-156.

In this article a professor at the Episcopal Divinity School in Cambridge, Massachusetts, speaks of her own decision to "come out." She says that for fifteen years she has been coming out sexually, experiencing attraction to women and to men. But she rejects the option of bisexuality because "coming out is the most radical, deeply personal and consciously political affirmation I can make on behalf of the possibilities of love and justice in the social order."

276. _____ . "Theological Explorations of Homosexuality." The Witness. Vol. 62, No. 6 (June 1979), pp. 12-15.

The transcript of a 1977 address in which Heyward discusses the spirituality of sexuality and challenges the use of the "categories" and "boxes" with which people tend to describe themselves and others in terms of sexuality. The author considers this a helpful forerunner to her article "Coming Out: Journey Without Maps" (No. 275).

277. Hiltner, Seward. "Kinsey and the Church." Journal of Sex Research. Vol. 8, No. 3 (August 1973), pp. 194-206.

An Alfred C. Kinsey Memorial Lecture given at Indiana University in May 1970 that describes and appraises the attitudes of church people toward Kinsey's books (see Nos. 101 and 102). The view is voiced that in practice the churches have come very close to accepting the bourgeois, romantic, and purely voluntaristic notion of sex relations. This means taking sex seriously in the sense of not being either casual or wholly puritanical about it.

278. Hinand, Gail. "One in Christ in His Church Today?" Trends. (July-August 1973), pp. 36-38.

At the time this article was published its author was codirector of a special project (Women in Leadership) of the Women's Program, United Presbyterian Church USA. She says at one point that she found more acceptance of gay persons at a party in the Hilton Hotel than at a special group before which she appeared at the Presbyterian General Assembly. Still, she will remain in Christianity and try to change it, since Christ died for all.

279. "Homosexuality." The New Columbia Encyclopedia, ed. by William H. Harris and Judith S. Levy (1975), p. 1263.

The article is totally neutral in tone, with more space being devoted to causation than to any other aspect of the subject. Includes a few references to the relationship between homosexuality and Western attitudes toward it.

280. "Homosexuality: A Re-Examination: E/SA Forum-60." Engage/Social Action. Vol. 8, No. 3 (March 1980), pp. 9-56.

A dozen mini-essays in the journal of the Board of Church and Society of the United Methodist Church. Together they comprise a variety of approaches to the issue, very much like the lead article by Edward Baumann, which explores a variety of perspectives, all of which lead up to an accepting stance. Includes brief annotated bibliography.

281. "Homosexuality: Biblical Guidance Through a Moral
       Morass." Christianity Today. Vol. 24, No. 8
       (April 18, 1980), pp. 488-489.

       Editorial statement by the nation's leading Evangelical
       journal declares that myths and a lack of clear teach-
       ing have blocked compassion on the one hand and
       discipline on the other.

282. Hooker, Evelyn. "Homosexuality" [under "Sexual Be-
       havior"]. International Encyclopedia of the Social
       Sciences, ed. by David Sills. Vol. 14 (1968), pp.
       222-232.

       There is brief mention of the Christian point of view
       in Western culture, followed by a purely scientific
       approach. Headings: etiology and determinants;
       psychodynamics of adult homosexuality; role differen-
       tiation and typology. Bibliography of forty entries.

283. Horner, Tom. "The Centurion's Servant." Insight: A
       Quarterly of Gay Catholic Opinion. Vol. 2, No. 3
       (Summer 1978), p. 9.

       A sermon on Matthew 8:5-13 as a possible homosex-
       ual reference. Horner uses the translations of The
       New English Bible and The New American Bible, both
       of which render pais as "boy" and suggests that Luke,
       in 7:1-10, changed pais to doulos, "slave," because
       of the particularly humanitarian emphasis that is
       found throughout his Gospel.

284. Humm, Andy, et al. "Silencing of Gay Issues in the
       Christian Churches." Insight: A Quarterly of
       Lesbian/Gay Christian Opinion. Vol. 3, No. 3 (Sum-
       mer 1979), pp. 5-13.

       This is a series of short articles on the same theme
       by various authors (in addition to Humm: Robert
       Nugent, Joan Clark, Michael Collins, Madge Rine-
       hardt, and John J. McNeill). Humm points out the
       discrepancy between the acceptance that the churches
       will offer in counsel and confessional versus what
       they are willing to stand up for in public. McNeill

writes on the personal consequences of eccesiastical obedience.

285. Humphreys, Laud. "Jesus Christ: A Sexual Person." Vector. Vol. 6, No. 12 (December 1970), pp. 13-14, 38.

286. Hyde, Clark, and Janet S. Hyde. "Homosexuality and the Theological Uses of Social Science: A Response to Ruth Tiffany Barnhouse." Anglican Theological Review. Vol. 59 (April 1977), pp. 187-190.

See Nos. 11 and 184.

287. "In the Matter of Joan L. Clark." Christianity and Crisis. Vol. 39, No. 10 (June 11, 1979), pp. 146-148.

This is an editorial in the form of a three-page article in defense of Joan L. Clark, who had just been dismissed from her employment with the Women's Division, Board of Global Ministries, United Methodist Church, after she had revealed her lesbianism. The editors find conflicts in this regard within the Methodist's own Book of Discipline, which was cited in connection with Clark's dismissal. See No. 209.

288. "International List of Gay Groups, Places, and Things." Motive. Vol. 32, No. 2 (1972), pp. 60-64.

List includes 314 items. This entire issue of Motive is devoted to the subject of homosexuality, as is No. 1 of this same volume. All of the articles, however (a total of nineteen in the two issues), seem a bit dated today.

289. Jackson, Dolores ("Dee"). "Prison Ministry," in Our Right to Love: A Lesbian Resource Book, ed. by Ginny Vida (Englewood Cliffs, New Jersey: Prentice-Hall, 1978), pp. 171-173.

This article by a Metropolitan Community Church

pastor tells of her efforts to carry out a prison ministry to homosexual women in Manhattan, Brooklyn,
and upstate New York.   She says that judges usually
give longer sentences to a woman who is a lesbian,
but generally women are not considered to be lesbian
unless they look "manly." Today's lesbian organizations offer help that was not available formerly.

290. Jackson, Don. "Testament of a Gay Militant," in The
New Gay Liberation Book: Writings and Photographs
About Gay (Men's) Liberation, ed. by Len Richmond and
Gary Noguera (Palo Alto, California: Ramparts, 1979),
pp. 23-31.

Jackson describes a number of incidents of homosexual oppression, and he attributes them expressly to
the negative attitude of the Judeo-Christian tradition.
The tone is bitter.

291. Jacobovits, Immanuel. "Homosexuality." Encyclopaedia Judaica. Vol. 8 (1971), pp. 961-962.

This article presents an overview of homosexual references in the postbiblical Jewish literature. It cites
the "virtual absence of homosexuality among Jews" at
the time as the reason for omission of any reference
to it in one important piece of literature (the Shulkhan
Arukh) but gives the Talmudic reference (Sotah 13b)
for the claim that the Egyptian Potiphar of the Book
of Genesis was homosexual. The article states that
homosexuality cannot be justified on any grounds.

292. Jennings, Theodore W. "Homosexuality and the Christian Faith: A Theological Reflection." The Christian
Century. Vol. 94, No. 5 (February 16, 1977), pp.
137-142.

Reprinted in Edward Batchelor, ed. Homosexuality
and Ethics, pp. 211-221 (No. 14).

293. Johnson, Dick. "Homosexuals and the Seminaries."
Engage/Social Action. Vol. 6, No. 8 (August 1978),
pp. 44-45.

294. Johnson, William R. "Protestantism and Gay Free-
     dom," in Positively Gay, ed. by Betty Berzon and
     Robert Leighton (Millbrae, California: Celestial
     Arts, 1979), pp. 65-78.

     United Church of Christ minister Bill Johnson was
     the first avowed homosexual candidate to be ordained
     in any denomination. He sees the current homophile
     movement as one of several historical challenges to
     religious freedom. The addresses of the Protestant
     denominational gay caucuses are listed at the end of
     the article.

295. Jones, Alan W. "Readers' Response: When Is a Ho-
     mosexual Not a Homosexual?" Anglican Theological
     Review. Vol. 59 (April 1977), pp. 183-186.

296. Jones, Clinton R. "Christopher Isherwood and the Re-
     ligious Quest," in The Gay Academic, ed. by Louie
     Crew (Palm Springs, California: ETC, 1978), pp.
     350-360.

     Though Isherwood is not a Christian, his novels show
     homosexual persons as those with the same feelings
     and emotions as heterosexual persons; thus, according
     to Canon Jones, Isherwood is helping those of homo-
     sexual orientation to find "a place of acceptance in
     Church and society."

297. Jones, Joe R. "Christian Sensibility with Respect to
     Homosexuality." Encounter. Vol. 40, No. 3 (Sum-
     mer 1979), pp. 209-221.

     Conceding the great difficulty of the topic, Jones still
     moves toward what he calls "the importance of Chris-
     tian sensibility of saying 'no' in the right way to ho-
     mosexuality." He argues not from biblical injunction,
     however, but from the standpoint of fulfillment in
     heterosexuality and of the distortion of it in homo-
     sexuality. Nevertheless, "the homosexual does not
     stand under any special condemnation from God."

298. Jones, W. Paul. "Homosexuality and Marriage: Ex-

ploring on the Theological Edge." Pastoral Psychology. Vol. 21, No. 209 (December 1970), pp. 29-37.

299. Karlen, Arno. "The Homosexual Heresy." Chaucer
Review. Vol. 6, No. 1 (1971), pp. 44-63.

300. Katz, Robert L. "Notes on Religious History, Attitudes, and Laws Pertaining to Homosexuality," in
NIMH Task Force on Homosexuality: Final Report
and Background Papers (Rockville, Maryland: National Institute of Mental Health, 1972), pp. 58-62.

301. Kavanagh, Julia [pseud.]. "My Son Is Gay." U.S.
Catholic. Vol. 45, No. 6 (June 1980), pp. 14-15.

This intimate revelation by a mother refers to loving
and unloving remarks she has heard from the lips of
priests. She wonders why some of them who wish
to address themselves to the subject of homosexuality
publicly do not undergo more pastoral counseling
courses beforehand. She admits not approving of homosexuality itself but accepts the fact of its
existence--and loves the person who may be homosexual.

302. Kelly, J. "The Aging Male Homosexual." The Geron-
tologist. Vol. 17, No. 4 (August 1970), pp. 328-332.

303. Kelsey, Morton T. "The Homosexual and the Church,"
in Sex: Thoughts for Contemporary Christians, ed.
by Michael J. Taylor (Garden City, New York:
Doubleday, 1972), pp. 221-243.

Parts of this essay may seem a bit dated today;
nevertheless it is provocative and well written. Sample comment: "Some of the rebellious teen-agers of
our society who are involved in violence are over-
compensating for their unconscious homosexual feelings." Kelsey comments on the biblical material as
well as the work on C. V. Jung in relation to homosexuality.

304. Kepner, Jim. "Gays and Religion." The Advocate. No. 118 (August 15, 1973), pp. 37, 39.

The secrets of the Mark fragment (the Secret Gospel of Mark) and other Gnostic texts for gay Christians. See Nos. 147 and 148 above. (Reprinted in Kepner's Gay Essays, a work that is not easy to find--hence not listed in this bibliography.)

305. _____. "God Met on Hoover Street." In Touch. No. 22 (February-March 1976), pp. 56-59.

On the Church of ONE Brotherhood and other gay religious groups.

306. Kosgela, Roger. "Open Doors to Gays: Grounds for Separation." Christianity Today. Vol. 20 (March 1976), p. 53.

307. Krody, Nancy. "An Open Lesbian Looks at the Church." Foundations: Baptist Journal of History and Theology. Vol. 20, No. 2 (April-June 1977), pp. 148-162.

This is a frank discussion of the turmoil going on in the lives of lesbians in the seminaries and in the congregations. Krody asks: "Why do I stay in the church which has oppressed me and my sisters and gay brothers?" Answer: "Because I believe what it taught me about God and love and grace and re-demption and justice. I want to see the church live up to its best self in God's name."

308. _____. "Woman, Lesbian, Feminist, Christian." Christianity and Crisis. Vol. 37, Nos. 9-10 (May 30-June 13, 1977), pp. 131-136 (combined issue).

This is an adaptation of the article by the same au-thor from the April-June 1977 issue of Foundations (No. 307).

309. Kuehnelt-Leddhin, Erik von. "The Problem of Homo-

sexuality: A Christian View." The Human Life Review. Vol. 4, No. 2 (Spring 1978), pp. 61-75.

310. Lamm, Harold. "The New Dispensation on Homosexuality: A Jewish Reaction to a Developing Christian Attitude." Jewish Life. Vol. 35, No. 3 (1968), pp. 11-16.

Lamm generally decries the softening Christian attitude toward homosexuality and hopes that it does not infect Judaism. He sees only two references in the Old Testament (Genesis 19 and Judges 19) but reports that Jewish tradition says the Egyptian Potiphar acquired Joseph from the Ishmaelites for homosexual purposes.

311. Larsen, Paul E., et al. "Christian Answers on Homosexuality. Journal of the American Scientific Affiliation. Vol. 31, No. 1 (1979), pp. 48-53.

312. Lee, Ronald R. "Ministering to the Homosexual." Explor. Vol. 1, No. 2 (Fall 1975), pp. 71-77.

313. Legg, W. Dorr. "A Moral Imperative." ONE Magazine. Vol. 11, No. 12 (December 1963), pp. 6-11.

314. "Lesbians and Politics: A Group Discussion." Radical Religion. Vol. 3, No. 2 (1977), pp. 44-51.

315. Lindsell, Harold. "Homosexuals and the Church." Christianity Today. Vol. 17, No. 25 (September 1973), pp. 8-12 (1288-1292).

If the biblical commandments about homosexuality are set aside and homosexuality is viewed only as a variant lifestyle, then other "sinners" can use the same logic to justify their own aberrations. The Church cannot admit those whom God excludes, says Lindsell.

316. Lovelace, Richard F. "The Active Homosexual Life-

style and the Church." Church and Society. Vol.
67, No. 5 (May-June 1977), pp. 12-23.

Lovelace argues that sexual reorientation is both
possible and desirable. The Church, he says, should
avoid the easy solutions either of homophobic rejection or of concession to the gay lifestyle (as an acceptable alternative) and "seek with all its energies
for a level of renewal and reformation." This article was expanded into a book a year later. See No.
111.

317. McGraw, James R. "Anita and the Gays." Christianity and Crisis. Vol. 37, No. 11 (June 27, 1977),
pp. 147-149.

McGraw points out that many see Anita Bryant and
her crusade as "just about the best thing that ever
happened for the politicization and 'uncloseting' of
gay people." He says that future "Gay Liberation
Day" celebrations and activist participation will test
this hypothesis.

318. _____ . "The Scandal of Peculiarity." Christianity
and Crisis. Vol. 36, No. 6 (April 16, 1973), pp.
63-68.

Readers are given a synopsis of two recent television
programs that presented homosexuality as illness and
abnormality, respectively. Such programs, McGraw
says, reinforce homosexual abhorrence on the part
of society and self-hatred among those most in need
of acceptance. His conclusion is that "gay people in
this country, all 20 million of us," must work for
nothing less than the same rights and dignities accorded all others.

319. McGuire, B. P. "Love, Friendship and Sex in the
Eleventh Century: The Experience of Anselm."
Studia Theologica. Vol. 28, No. 2 (1974), pp. 111-
152.

320. McNaught, Brian. "Gay and Catholic," in Positively

Gay, ed. by Betty Berzon and Robert Leighton (Millbrae, California: Celestial Arts, 1979), pp. 56-64.

America's best-known gay Catholic journalist tells what it is like to be Catholic and homosexual in today's society.

321. McNeill, John. "The Homosexual and the Church." National Catholic Reporter. Vol. 9, No. 38 (October 5, 1973), pp. 7-8, 13-14.

This is a preview of the arguments that Fr. McNeill later presented in detail in his book The Church and the Homosexual (No. 114).

322. Marney, Carlyle. "The Christian Community and the Homosexual." Religion in Life. Vol. 35, No. 5 (1966), pp. 760-773.

323. Marty, Don. "The Church and the Homosexuals." The Christian Herald. Vol. 101, No. 1 (January 1978), pp. 42-45, 47-49.

324. Matt, Herschel J. "Sin, Crime, Sickness, or Alternative Life Style? A Jewish Approach to Homosexuality." Judaism: A Quarterly of Jewish Life and Thought. Vol. 27 (Winter 1978), pp. 13-24.

Matt says that Jews teach that we should judge not, until we have walked a mile in the other person's shoes. But homosexuality poses a problem for Judaism, Matt writes, because of the centrality of the family in its tradition. Nevertheless, he urges compassion.

324a. Maynor, Joe E. "Fundamentalist Ministers vs. Gay Rights Groups." TV Guide. Vol. 28, No. 46 (November 15-21, 1980), pp. 16-20.

A clash between fundamentalist ministers and gay-rights groups in Charlotte, North Carolina, and Dallas, Texas, could lead to an acid test for the fairness doctrine in television broadcasting. The article documents a station's giving free time for a gay pastor to answer attacks on gays and tells of other anti-gay programs being canceled. It notes that this whole issue is being carefully watched by the FCC.

325. Meeks, John E. "Should Homosexuals Lead Youth Groups?" Engage/Social Action. Vol. 3, No. 5 (May 1975), pp. 32-33.

326. Mehler, Barry. "Gay Jews." Moment. Vol. 2 (February-March 1977), pp. 22ff.

327. Meic, Robert K. "Sexuality and Human Community." Christopher Street. Vol. 4, No. 11 (July-August 1980), pp. 8-10.

Meic castigates the Roman Catholic Church for its stance on all matters sexual: "The errors of Christian teachings on sexuality, especially from the See of Peter, are as pernicious as they are widespread." If it continues to remain numb to "the vibrant strength that human sexuality imparts to human community," the Church itself will be the loser.

328. Milhaven, John G. "Homosexuality and the Christian." Homiletic and Pastoral Review. Vol. 68, No. 8 (May 1968), pp. 663-669.

329. Miller, Rhea Y. "Two Stones and One Bird: Religion and the Lesbian," in Our Right to Love: A Lesbian Resource Book, ed. by Ginny Vida (Englewood Cliffs, New Jersey: Prentice-Hall, 1978), pp. 167-171.

This article by a Metropolitan Community Church pastor tries to explain to her sister lesbians what organized religion has to say to them today. She says that there is really "no place for the lesbian to lay her head, but there are plenty of places to dig in." As for her, she must keep in touch with "the Reality of loving and being loved" (implying belief in a Divine Being).

330. Mollenkott, Virginia Ramey. "Joyful Worship in the Midst of Danger." The Christian Century. Vol. 96 (September 26, 1979), p. 910.

Mollenkott describes here a national conference that she attended of the Universal Fellowship of Metropolitan Community Churches in Los Angeles, August 19, 1979. She says that despite numerous bomb threats, the meeting went on, with much evangelical hymn-singing and an old-fashioned gospel sermon. She reflects upon worshiping "among a persecuted people" and asks others to cease "building walls of hostility."

331. _____, and Letha Scanzoni. "Homosexuality: It's Not As Simple as We Think." Faith/at/Work. Vol. 91, No. 3 (April 1978), pp. 8, 10, 18.

332. Muelder, Walter G. "Approaches to 'Homosexuality' and Their Implications for Ministry." Explor. Vol. 1, No. 2 (Fall 1975), pp. 28-51.

333. Mugavero, Francis J. "Sexuality--God's Gift: Pastoral Letter of the Most Reverend Francis J. Mugavero, Bishop of Brooklyn, February 11, 1976." Insight: A Quarterly of Gay Catholic Opinion. Vol. 1, No. 3 (Spring 1977), pp. 5-7.

This is a reprint of the bishop's pastoral letter from the Brooklyn Tablet. It is a response to the controversial December 29, 1975, Vatican statement entitled "Declaration on Certain Questions Concerning Sexual Ethics." Bishop Mugavero speaks of homosexual orientation but not of "homosexuals," of "persons" rather than of stereotypes.

334. Murdoch, Iris. "The Moral Decision About Homosexuality." ONE Magazine. Vol. 12, No. 11 (1964), pp. 6-10.

Not seen; but in regard to its possible stance, note that Murdoch has one strongly pro-gay novel, A Fairly Honourable Defeat (Penguin, 1972).

335. National Council of Churches of Christ in the U.S.A.
Commission on Faith and Order. "A Call to Re-
sponsible Ecumenical Debate on Controversial Issues:
Abortions and Homosexuality." Ecumenical Trends.
Vol. 8, No. 3 (March 1979), pp. 45-48.

This study document approaches both abortion and
homosexuality as major social issues and explores
areas in which Christian responses to them might be
channeled. (If ordered through the National Council's
Commission on Faith and Order [475 Riverside Drive,
New York, NY 10027], an update on recent denominational action may be included with a copy of the article.)

336. Nelson, James B. "Homosexuality and the Church:
Towards a Sexual Ethics of Love." Christianity and
Crisis. Vol. 37, No. 5 (April 4, 1977), pp. 63-69.

Nelson reviews what some of the theologians, e.g.,
Barth (see No. 13) and Thielicke (see No. 157), have
said on the subject and presents some explanation of
the biblical evidence. He says the Bible did not
know about the homosexual condition--hence it con-
demns only such acts committed by those who are
"presumed to be heterosexually constituted." Reprinted as "Homosexuality and the Church" in St.
Luke's Journal of Theology. Vol. 22, No. 3 (June
1979), pp. 197-211.

337. Nicholi, Armand D., II. "Homosexualism and Homosexuality." Baker's Dictionary of Christian Ethics,
ed. by Carl F. H. Henry (Grand Rapids, Michigan:
Baker, 1973), pp. 295-297.

Four and one-half columns discuss the subject in
general terms and conclude: "Those who base their
faith on the OT and NT documents cannot doubt that
their strong prohibitions of homosexual behavior make
homosexual activity a direct transgression of God's
law."

338. Novak, Michael. "Gay Is Not Liberation." Commonweal. No. 100 (1974), pp. 318-319.

Traditional viewpoint. There are responses in issue
No. 102.

339. _____. "Men Without Women." Human Life Review. Vol. 5, No. 1 (Winter 1979), pp. 61-67.

340. Oaks, Robert F. "'Things Fearful to Name': Sodomy and Buggery in Seventeenth Century New England," in The American Man, ed. by Elizabeth H. and Joseph H. Pleck (Englewood Cliffs, New Jersey: Prentice-Hall, 1980).

341. Oliver, Kay, and Wayne Christianson. "Unhappily 'Gay': From Closet to the Front Page." Moody Monthly. Vol. 78, No. 5 (January 1978), pp. 62-68.

342. Orbach, W. "Homosexuality and Jewish Law." Journal of Family Law. Vol. 14 (1976), pp. 353-381.

343. Osborn, Ronald E. "Ordination for Homosexuals? A Negative Answer Qualified by Some Reflections." Encounter. Vol. 40, No. 3 (Summer 1979), pp. 245-263.

344. Patterson, Ben. "A Belated Answer: Editorial." The Wittenburg Door. No. 39 (October-November 1977), pp. 18-19, 22-25.

This five-page treatise is less an editorial than a position paper. Patterson sees homosexuality as clearly forbidden by scripture. Though he acknowledges homosexual orientation, he says that the homosexual Christian must make a complete break with homosexual acts. "We [heterosexual Christians] should be demanding: but in love, not in judgment."

345. Pattison, E. Mansell; Stanley Hauerwas; and John Patton. "Understanding Homosexuality: A Symposium." Pastoral Psychology. Vol. 24 (Spring 1976), pp. 231-244.

346. Peron, Jim. "The Christian Counselor and Homosexual Patient." CAPS Bulletin. Vol. 5, No. 2 (1979), pp. 18-20.

For the same article in pamphlet form see Peron, No. 435.

347.　Pinney, Gregory W. "A Welcome to (Not) All Per-
　　　sons." The Witness. Vol. 61, No. 10 (October
　　　1978), pp. 10-13.

This is the story about a Methodist congregation in
the Midwest that was located squarely in the middle
of a homosexual neighborhood; yet it refused to rent
space to the Metropolitan Community Church, a homosexually orientated denomination--space that had
been regularly rented to secular groups. Gay persons did not feel welcome in the church itself, says
this author.

348.　Pittenger, [W.] Norman. "Homosexuality and the
　　　Christian Tradition." Christianity and Crisis. Vol.
　　　34, No. 14 (August 5, 1974), pp. 178-181.

Pittenger says here that there is not much point in
citing at length from the Old and New Testament references, although he then proceeds to discuss some
of them in general terms. More interested in a theological approach to homosexuality he has published
thus far at least four books in this area (see Nos.
130-133).

349.　_____. "A Theological Approach to Understanding
　　　Homosexuality." Religion in Life. Vol. 43 (Winter
　　　1974), pp. 436-444; rpt. in Male and Female (see
　　　No. 12).

As in earlier works (see No. 348), Pittenger does
not make great use of the biblical material--although
he mentions some of it, highlighting I John 4. Christians are to love God, he says, "but their loving God
is expressed practically and immediately in a loving
relationship with other human beings."

350.　Poole, Lee. "The Catholic Homosexual." New Black-
　　　friars. Vol. 56 (November 1975), pp. 500-505.

351. Pope, Marvin H. "Homosexuality." Interpreter's Dictionary of the Bible. Supplementary Volume (Nashville, Tennessee: Abingdon, 1976), pp. 415-417.

All one has to do is to compare this article with the one of the same title in the 1962 volume of this dictionary to see how thinking has changed in this area. There is much more interest in the subject here. Pope discusses the principal biblical references and, to a certain extent, some of the related Middle Eastern materials. There is also a bibliography.

352. Powell, John R. "Understanding Male Homosexuality: Developmental Recapitulation in a Christian Perspective." Journal of Psychology and Theology. Vol. 2, No. 3 (Summer 1974), pp. 163-173.

Reviews etiological explanations for male homosexuality and biblical teachings regarding marriage and the family. A concept of "developmental recapitulation" as a means of guiding therapy is discussed and related to a mode of multiple therapy with male clients having homosexual concerns.

353. Prescott, Anne Lake. "English Writers and Beza's Latin Epigrams." Studies in the Renaissance. Vol. 21 (1974), pp. 83-117.

Theodore de Beze, or Beza, was successor to John Calvin, translator of scriptures, and author of eccesiastical treatises, but in his youth he wrote some Latin love poetry. This caused him to be accused of lechery and homosexuality. These attacks on his personal life were often linked to critics of his doctrinal positions by Roman Catholics and Lutherans.

354. Rabinowitz, Seymour. "Developmental Problems in Catholic Seminarians." Psychiatry. Vol. 32, No. 1 (1969), pp. 107-117.

Discusses observations made in diagnostic, evaluative, and therapeutic work with twenty-five Catholic seminarians. Says they exhibited three types of psychopathology: (1) homosexuality, (2) psychophysiology and related responses, and (3) depression. Some unique problems in the psychiatric treatment of seminarians are discussed.

355. Rash, John P. "Reforming Pastoral Attitudes Toward Homosexuality." Union Seminary Quarterly Review. Vol. 25, No. 4 (Summer 1970), pp. 439-455.

Homosexuality and heterosexuality are equally valid sexual adaptations. Three major objections to homosexuality are discussed and counterarguments are presented. Homosexuality is susceptible neither to "behavioral" nor to "psychoanalytic" therapy and neither should be attempted.

356. Rechy, John. "An Open Letter to Anita Bryant," in The New Gay Liberation Book: Writings and Photographs About Gay (Men's) Liberation, ed. by Len Richmond and Gary Noguera (Palo Alto, California: Ramparts, 1979), pp. 213-219.

In regard to the June 7, 1977, Dade County (Florida) referendum, Rechy accuses Bryant of not being religious but anti-religious. He says that homosexual persons have had enough persecution and vows that they will fight back. The style is highly literary.

357. Rickards, Frank S. "Victims of Society." CR: A Quarterly of the Community of the Resurrection. No. 308 (Easter 1980), pp. 18-24. Reprinted from Nursing Mirror (November 1, 1979).

This article (in a Church of England religious journal) begins with the Kinsey Report and other references to the extent of homosexuality in society. It then surveys what has taken place since 1948. Conclusion: "The most sensitive index of any civilisation is the esteem and care it has for its non-violent minorities. The time seems appropriate for the full acceptance of the homosexual minority by the heterosexual majority."

358. Ross, John C., and John M. Gessell. "Report on the

Documentation Program on Diocesan and Other Materials in the Area of Human Sexuality." St. Luke's Journal of Theology. Vol. 22, No. 3 (June 1979), pp. 212-216.

Despite the title the major concern of this article is homosexuality. It reviews what various Episcopal dioceses have done in the area of sex education between that denomination's Minneapolis convention (1976) and its Denver one (1979). More than half of the article is taken up with an annotated bibliography.

359. Ross, M. W. "Exorcism as Pyschiatric Treatment: A Homosexual Case Study." Archives of Sexual Behavior. Vol. 8, No. 4 (July 1979), pp. 379-383.

360. Roth, Wolfgang. "What of Sodom and Gomorrah? Homosexual Acts in the Old Testament." Explor. Vol. 1, No. 2 (Fall 1975), pp. 7-14.

Roth says that the men of Sodom and Gomorrah--and also Gibeah--are condemned primarily because they break covenant (between host and guest) and also destroy community. The Levitical texts proscribe homosexual acts because the latter work against cultic unity. Roth makes use here of anthropologist Mary Douglas and her concepts of pollution and taboo.

361. Rudolph, Sylvia. "One of Our Family Is Gay." Christian Home. Vol. 9, No. 9 (Fall 1975), pp. 15-19.

This article discusses from a neutral point of view a dilemma that faces a great many American families. Christian Home is United Methodism's family magazine.

362. Sample, Robert L., and Randy Akers. "Homosexuality in Ancient Greece and in the Christian Middle Ages." Explor. Vol. 1, No. 2 (Fall 1975), pp. 15-19.

The extremely liberal attitude of the ancient Greeks toward homosexuality is reviewed and found to be in total contrast to the restrictive medieval stance, which is the source of our modern heritage in this regard.

363. Sandmire, James E. "Accepting My Uniqueness." Trends. (July-August 1973), pp. 27-29.

This is a highly personal confessional by a pastor in the Metropolitan Community Church, though it appears in a now-defunct magazine of the United Presbyterian Board of Education. The author is homosexual and makes no excuses for it, although in the review of his life history he tells how strongly he had tried to resist it--and failed. There are questions for discussion.

364. Scanzoni, Letha. "Conservative Christians and Gay Civil Rights." The Christian Century. Vol. 93, No. 32 (October 13, 1976), pp. 857-862.

When a gay civil-rights bill was passed by the City Council of Bloomington, Indiana, in December 1975, there was an outcry from conservative religious groups. This article documents in some detail the heated controversy.

365. Schaibley, Robert W. "An Evaluation of the Australian Lutheran 'Statement on Homosexuality.'" Concordia Theological Quarterly. Vol. 42, No. 1 (January 1978), pp. 1-7.

366. Schindler, Ruben. "Homosexuality, the Halacha, and the Helping Professions." Journal of Religion and Health. Vol. 18 (April 1979), pp. 132-138.

367. Scott, David A. "Ordaining a Homosexual Person: A Policy Proposal." St. Luke's Journal of Theology. Vol. 22, No. 3 (June 1979), pp. 185-196.

Scott makes three recommendations: (1) that bishops should not ordain persons whose teaching and behavior would present homosexual genital activity as an

alternative Christian lifestyle; (2) that bishops may
ordain those of homosexual orientation if these persons would not, by example or teaching, represent
homosexual genital actions as a normative alternative;
and (3) that the Episcopal Church in General Convention leave the question of ordination to the individual
dioceses.

368. "Seminar on Hedonistic Sex, Mutual Affection Sex, and
Bible Sex." Religious Education. Vol. 65, No. 2
(March 1970), pp. 170-176.

A report from the Religious Education Association's
annual convention. The concensus was that attitudes
toward homosexuality as a depraved and perverse
state do not help individuals. Although a minority
held that celibates probably could not live a fulfilled
life, the majority accepted the possibility of person-
ality fulfillment in celibacy that is lived within a
framework of giving service to others.

369. Shelp, Earl E. "Pastor, I Think I'm Gay." The
Christian Ministry. Vol. 10, No. 2 (March 1979),
pp. 18-19.

370. Shinn, Roger L., "Persecution of the Homosexual."
Christianity and Crisis. Vol. 10, No. 2 (May 2,
1966), pp. 84-85.

371. Shoemaker, Dennis E. "Getting Straight About Gays."
Trends. (July-August 1973), pp. 20-26.

A heterosexual writer for the United Presbyterian
Board of Education attended a symposium sponsored
by the San Francisco-based Council on Religion and
the Homosexual and in this article gives readers his
impressions. He explains how attending the symposium exploded some of his own ideas about homosexual stereotypes. There are questions for discussion at the end.

372. Siegel, Paul. "Homophobia: Types, Origins, and

Remedies." Christianity and Crisis. Vol. 39, No.
17 (November 12, 1979), pp. 208-284.

Presents the results of several experiments on homophobia conducted by professional psychologists. The
most homophobic were those who feared that "there
but for the grace of God go I!" Again, many people
display prejudice against someone who is known to
be homosexual, whereas they would not be prejudiced
against that same person if he or she were not known
to be homosexual. Reveals statistics that show that
75 percent of those surveyed were opposed to homosexual clergy in 1970 but only 54 percent were opposed to them in 1977.

373. Sims, Bennett J. "Sex and Homosexuality: A Pastoral
Statement." Christianity Today. Vol. 22, No. 10
(February 24, 1978), pp. 23-30.

The well-known Episcopal bishop of Atlanta, who has
been quite outspoken on the subject of homosexuality,
presents here his views against it. The substance
of this article, which received wide reprint circula-
tion, is sometimes referred to as the "Sims Report."

374. Smedes, Lewis B. "Homosexuality: Sorting Out the
Issues." The Reformed Journal. Vol. 28, No. 1
(January 1978), pp. 9-12.

375. _____. "The San Diego Decision: Presbyterians
and Homosexuality." The Reformed Journal. Vol.
28, No. 8 (August 1978), pp. 12-16.

376. Smith, Dwight C., Jr. "Presbyterians on Homosexuality: Studying 'Others,' Finding Self." Christianity
and Crisis. Vol. 38, No. 2 (February 20, 1978),
pp. 22-27.

By studying homosexuality as a member of the United
Presbyterian Task Force this writer says that he
overcame his curiosity about the subject and in the
process rediscovered his own heterosexuality. He
suggests that the Presbyterians "put pluralism to

work for the Kingdom" rather than use pluralism as
a battlefield for ideological supremacy.

377.   Smith, R. W.   "Research and Homosexuality."   The
        Humanist.   Vol. 38, No. 2 (March-Spring 1978), pp.
        20-22.

        The emphasis of society is upon conformity.   There
        is a discussion of Stanley Schacter's research on hu-
        man reactions to deviance, and the model is applied
        to homosexuality.   "Because we are so encultured in
        a heterosexual mode of perceiving and behaving, we
        may learn, by about the age of three or four, to call
        anybody we dislike a 'queer' or 'fag.'"   It is difficult
        for even the best researchers to be objective on the
        subject.   Brief bibliography.

378.   Snow, John Hall.   "Gay People and Parish Life."   The
        Witness.   Vol. 61, No. 10 (October 1978), pp. 4-9.

        Snow discusses the predicament of the gay person (or
        persons) in the actual parish situation--from the
        standpoint of the congregation's knowing or not know-
        ing about the individual's homosexuality.   The author
        is professor of pastoral theology at the Episcopal
        Divinity School in Cambridge, Massachusetts.

379.   Solheim, James E.   "She's Still Our Daughter."   A.D.
        Vol. 8, No. 5 (May 1979), pp. 31-32.

        Tells how an Oregon couple came to grips with their
        daughter's homosexuality.   Finding it difficult to ac-
        cept at first, they came little by little to be suppor-
        tive of their daughter.   For quite some time after
        they first learned of it they were "closeted" parents;
        today they are activists for both local and statewide
        gay causes.

380.   Souster, Howard.   "Data Sheet on Homosexuality."   Ep-
        worth Review.   Vol. 7, No. 2 (May 1979), pp. 22-25.

        Attitudes, causation, and the role of the churches are
        the three topics discussed in this article in a Method-

ist publication. The conclusion is that "the Church possesses the opportunity to play the most constructive role of any agency concerned with homosexuals as persons." There is a brief annotated bibliography compiled by Dr. James Seakins.

381. Springer, R. "Holy God, Gays Want In." Today's Parish. Vol. 12 (January 1980), pp. 10-13.

382. Stoll, James. "Unitarian-Universalist Association Passes Liberalized Policy Statement." Vector. Vol. 6, No. 9 (September 1970), pp. 22-23.

383. Stoller, Robert J. "Sexual Deviation." Encyclopaedia Britannica, 15 ed. Vol. 16 (1974), pp. 601-610.

There are four classifications of deviations: (1) homosexuality; (2) deviations focusing on gender identity; (3) those focusing on special patterns of acts; and (4) others. For (1) above it says that treatment is by psychoanalysis or related psychotherapies, as others "have all failed." The article "Homosexuality" in the index volume (of the Micropaedia) is exceedingly brief.

384. Stoltenberg, John. "Toward Gender Justice," in For Men Against Sexism, ed. by John Snodgrass (Albion, California: Times Change, 1977), pp. 74-83.

Stoltenberg sees the context of Leviticus 18:22--"You must not lie with a man as with a woman"--as basically misogynist; for it is in the midst of a catalog of rules with two major emphases: men's property rights over the bodies of women and a loathing of a female carnality. The essay elaborates this dilemma and suggests how to overcome it. Bibliography.

385. "Symposium: Sexual Preference and Gender Identity." Hastings Law Journal. Vol. 30, No. 4 (March 1979).

This single issue of a law review should by all means be consulted by those concerned with the current sta-

tus of homosexuality and the law. The symposium
contains seven articles, the major one being "Our
Straight-Laced Judges: The Legal Position of Homosexual Persons in the United States," by Rhonda R.
Rivera. A shorter article, "Legal Homophobia and
the Christian Church," is by Ellen Barrett, the first
avowed homosexual candidate ordained in the Episcopal Church.

386. Tarachow, Sidney. "St. Paul and Early Christianity:
A Psychoanalytic and Historical Study," in Psychoanalysis and the Social Sciences, ed. by W. Muen-
sterberger. Vol. IV (New York: International Universities, 1955), pp. 223-281.

Romans 7:14 is quoted to point out that Paul's own
flesh was quite imperfectly suppressed, and I Corinthians 13 to show that he craved love. Tarachow
says that Paul had a need for male companionship,
not for women. "His ethics, his life and his theology
betray a strong, latent passive homosexuality."

387. Taylor, G. Rattray. "Historical and Mythological Aspects of Homosexuality," in Sexual Inversion: The
Multiple Roots of Homosexuality, ed. by Judd Marmor (New York: Basic Books, 1965), pp. 140-164.

Taylor says that we have the tendency to judge all
sexual behavior, including homosexuality, by the
standards of our own culture; hence our conclusions
about former societies have most often been wrong.
He discusses temple prostitution, gender-role changes,
and bisexuality in the ancient world.

388. Thompson, J. A. "The Significance of the Verb Love
in the David-Jonathan Narratives of I Samuel." Vetus
Testamentum, Vol. 24 (1974), pp. 334-338.

Thompson contends that the verb "love" in these narratives has political connotations, as in I Kings 5:1,
and that David's covenant with Jonathan here must be
seen as one in a long line of steps in which the author of I-II Samuel narrates David's movement to the
throne.

389. Trumbach, Randolph. "London's Sodomites: Homosexual Behavior and Western Culture in the 18th Century." Journal of Social History. Vol. 11, No. 1 (Fall 1977), pp. 1-33.

The homosexual subculture of the eighteenth century greatly resembled that of the twentieth but with one major difference: no organized group, other than occasional religious revivalists, threatened the exposure of homosexuals, whereas a "psychology of deviance" and an efficient police force oppress the twentieth-century homosexual.

390. Unsworth, Richard P. "Theological Table-Talk: Human Sexuality." Theology Today. Vol. 36 (April 1979), pp. 36, 58-65.

391. Wagenaar, Theodore C., and Patricia E. Bartos. "Orthodoxy and Attitudes of Clergymen Towards Homosexuality and Abortion." Review of Religious Research. Vol. 18, No. 2 (Winter 1977), pp. 114-125.

Attitudes of clergy toward homosexuality and abortion are examined vis-à-vis two main variables: orthodoxy and the often-experienced contradictory implications of the moral and the civil views of the clergy. Clergy with a less unidimensional approach to life, those who distinguish between what they feel is right from a moral, religious standpoint and what is right from a civil standpoint, are the most accepting of the two social issues.

392. Wagner, Roman. "Moving into Uncharted Territory." Counseling and Values. Vol. 22, No. 3 (April 1978), pp. 184-196.

"Institutionally," writes Wagner, "the Christian Churches are still in the 'dark ages' concerning the issue of gay ministry." Two models for ministry are presented in brief, followed by some of the author's own suggestions for counselors. Brief bibliography.

393. Ward, Michael, and Mark Freeman. "Defending Gay

Rights: The Campaign Against the Briggs Amendment in California." Radical American. Vol. 13, No. 4 (1979), pp. 11-26.

The successful campaign in November 1978 against the Briggs Amendment in the state of California (to bar homosexual teachers from employment) signified an argument in favor of a grass-roots approach to organizing. The groups that made up the coalition against the amendment are discussed.

394. Ward, W. Ralph. "United Methodists Won't Ordain Homosexuals." United Methodists Today/Today's Ministry Section. Vol. 2, No. 6 (June 1975), pp. 77-83.

The bishop of the New York area of the United Methodist Church says no to homosexual ordinations.

395. Watts, Alan. "No More Armed Clergymen," in The New Gay Liberation Book: Writings and Photographs About Gay (Men's) Liberation, ed. by Len Richmond and Gary Noguera (Palo Alto, California: Ramparts, 1979), pp. 143-146.

Both the Jewish and Christian communities, Watts says, should be castigated for the part that they might have played in any form of sexual oppression. Though heterosexually orientated himself, the author says that he sees nothing wrong with any expression of human sexuality as long as no one is hurt by it.

396. Way, Peggy. "Homosexual Counseling as a Learning Ministry." Christianity and Crisis. Vol. 37, Nos. 9-10 (May 30-June 13, 1977), pp. 123-131 (combined issue).

This complex article is not easy to summarize, but basically Way says that counselors must learn to work with all persons in need of help, regardless of their genital orientation. She lists and tries to answer five questions that are most often addressed to her in regard to homosexual persons. She calls this her "Ministry to Straights." Her "Ministry to Gays" is defined mostly in terms of struggle.

397. Weber, Joseph C. "Does the Bible Condemn Homosexual Acts?" Engage/Social Action. Vol. 3, No. 5
(May 1975), pp. 28-31, 34-35.

Weber follows D. S. Bailey's exegesis of the Sodom
story as a breach of hospitality rather than as attempted homosexual rape (see No. 7). His exegesis
of the Pauline references to homosexuality, however,
is entirely his own and should be consulted by anyone
researching the subject in Paul.

398. White, Richard. "When Homosexuality Hits a Marriage:
His Story." Christian Life. Vol. 40, No. 2 (June
1978), pp. 24, 51-54.

399. White, Rosalie. "When Homosexuality Hits a Marriage:
Her Story." Christian Life. Vol. 40, No. 2 (June
1978), pp. 25, 55-58.

400. Williams, Lewis. "The Churches: Where They Stand
Today." Vector. Vol. 7, No. 8 (August 1971), pp.
24-25, 35, 44-45.

401. Wink, Walter. "Biblical Perspectives on Homosexuality." The Christian Century. Vol. 96, No. 36 (November 7, 1979), pp. 1082-1086.

After reviewing a number of untenable Old Testament
regulations, Wink concludes that the Bible has no
sexual ethic but "only a love ethic which is constantly
being brought to bear on whatever sexual mores are
dominant in any given country, or culture, or period." Furthermore, the Gospel's attitude toward the
oppressed, he says, is unmistakably clear and positive. See, also, reader's response in the January
2-9, 1980, issue, pp. 20-25.

402. Wood, Robert [W.]. "Sex Life in Ancient Civilizations,"
in The Encyclopedia of Sexual Behavior, ed. by Albert Ellis and Albert Abarnabel (New York: Hawthorn, 1961), Vol. I, pp. 119-131.

Several pages are devoted to the sexual practices of ancient Greece, several pages to Rome, and the same for Israel and India. The treatment of homosexuality within the first three cultures is relevant to the homosexual references in the Bible. There is a useful bibliography of works dealing with the ancient sources.

403. _____. "Homosexual Behavior in the Bible." ONE Institute Quarterly. Vol. 5, No. 1 (1962), pp. 10-19.

Wood discusses the David-Jonathan story as a probable homosexual reference, and the same for Ruth and Naomi. The discussion of the other biblical material is well organized and scholarly. There are some suggestions of appropriate texts for preaching purposes.

404. Woods, Richard, et al. "Toward a Gay Christian Ethic." Insight: A Quarterly of Lesbian/Gay Catholic Opinion. Vol. 3, No. 2 (Spring-Summer 1979), pp. 5-12.

Several writers (other than Woods: Mary Hunt, Gregory Baum, Norman Pittenger, Michael Collins, and Peter Grammon) each contribute short articles on the same topic: ways of conducting oneself as an ethical person and at the same time as a person who is homosexual. This is best expressed by becoming a loving person (Woods, Pittenger, especially).

405. Wright, Elliott. "The Church and Gay Liberation." Christian Century. Vol. 88, No. 9 (March 3, 1971), pp. 281-285.

This article reviews the unfolding of the homophile movement between June 1969 and the time of writing, including what steps the various denominations have taken in confronting the issue and what literature has been relevant to the movement as it pertains to the Church thus far. The article would be useful for those researching the years 1969-70.

406. Yorkston, Neil. "Lesbianism," in Baker's Dictionary

of Christian Ethics, ed. by Carl F. H. Henry (Grand Rapids, Michigan: Baker, 1973), p. 386.

Three paragraphs devoted to the traditional disapprobation.

407. Zlotlow, Moses. "Religious Rationalization of a Homosexual." New York State Journal of Medicine. Vol. 72, No. 22 (November 1972), pp. 2775-2778.

Reports the unusual case history of a homosexual male who used a religious rationalization in defense of his homosexuality. He claimed that Adam and Eve were expelled from paradise because of their heterosexuality and that it was a sin to have sexual relations with a woman. Bizarre.

III. PAMPHLETS AND PAPERS

---

408. Barnett, Walter. Homosexuality and the Bible: An
      Interpretation. Wallingford, Pennsylvania: Pendle
      Hill, 1979.

      This thirty-two-page monograph (in pamphlet format)
      is based on scholarship and a very strong conviction
      on the author's part to argue that the Bible does not
      condemn homosexuality as such. Contains a reference
      list of twenty-one items.

409. Blair, Ralph. An Evangelical Look at Homosexuality.
      New York: Privately printed, 1972. Available from
      the Homosexual Community Counseling Center, 30
      East 60 Street, New York, NY 10022.

      This twelve-page booklet argues for understanding and
      acceptance of homosexuality. It was written especial-
      ly from the Evangelical Christian point of view.
      There is some exegesis of the Pauline references
      followed by pragmatic arguments and a rather emo-
      tional appeal from Reverend Troy Perry of the Metro-
      politan Community Church. First published as "The
      Gay Evangelical" in Homosexuality and Religion (No.
      13) in the Otherwise Monograph Series of the National
      Task Force on Student Personnel Services and Homo-
      sexuality.

410. _____. Holier-Than-Thou Hocus-Pocus and Homo-

sexuality. New York: Privately printed, 1977. Available from the Homosexual Community Counseling Center, 30 East 60 Street, New York, NY 10022.

A forty-eight-page pamphlet that attempts to reform the anti-homosexual attitudes of Evangelical Christians. In this booklet, as in some of his other writings, Blair discusses some of the homosexual "cures" and tries to show their position as untenable.

411.   . Homophobia in the Church. New York: Privately printed, 1979. Available from the Homosexual Community Counseling Center, 30 East 60 Street, New York, NY 10022.

This is a twenty-five-page pamphlet, with one page of references. Blair says that Christians who are homophobic, which is both a fear and loathing of homosexuality, misread their Bibles and their theology. The answer, he suggests, is getting back to a sound Christian ethic.

412. Blamires, David. Homosexuality from the Inside. London: Social Responsibility Council of the Religious Society of Friends, 1973.

413. Catholic Council for Church and Society (The Netherlands). Homosexual People in Society: A Contribution to the Dialogue Within the Faith Community. Trans. by Bernard A. Nachbar. Foreword by Gregory Baum. Mt. Rainier, Maryland: New Ways Ministry, 1980.

An official document of the Dutch bishops' Council for Church and Society, published with episcopal approval (in Dutch) in August 1979, Homosexual People in Society is, according to Gregory Baum, "one of the few ecclesiastical documents advocating a new approach and manifesting sympathy for homosexual people."

414. Chambers, Chester V. A Critique of the United Methodist Position on Homosexuality. Toledo, Ohio: Privately printed (by the author), 1975.

The Social Principles of the United Methodist Church
adopted in 1972 declared the practice of homosexuality
to be "incompatible with Christian teaching." This is
a forty-one-page piece issued prior to discussion of
this matter at the 1976 General Conference of the
United Methodist Church. It includes brief chapters
on homosexuality from the psychological, biblical,
theological, and ethical points of view, along with a
brief bibliography.

415. _____. Some Questions for Christians About Homosexuality. Toledo, Ohio: Privately printed (by the
author), 1980.

Answers to eleven questions about gay people addressed to United Methodists before they were to consider the gay issue at their 1950 General Conference.
Includes bibliography.

416. Dignity, Inc. Theological Pastoral Resources: A
Packet of Articles on Homosexuality from a Catholic
Perspective. San Diego, California: Privately printed,
1977 (5th ed.). Available from Dignity, Inc., Suite
11, 1500 Massachusetts Avenue, Washington, DC
20005.

This includes Dignity's "Statement of Position and
Purpose"; several articles by Roman Catholic priests
and lay persons, including Brian McNaught's "The
Sad Dilemma of the Gay Catholic"; and contributions
by Norman Pittenger and John McNeill. Although
called a packet, this is really a single pamphlet.

417. Disciples of Christ. Homosexuality and the Church: A
Study Packet. Indianapolis, Indiana: Privately
printed, 1979. Available from Department of Christian Education, Christian Church (Disciples of Christ),
P.O. Box 1986, Indianapolis, IN 46206.

A packet of materials, including Use Guide, Study
Document issued by this denomination's General Assembly of 1977, a Spectrum of Opinion (on Homosexuality), Annotated Bibliography, Attitudes and Assumptions Check List, and Actions of the General Assem-

bly Concerning Civil Liberties (1977) and Concerning Ordination (1979).

418. Fairchild, Betty. The Church's Ministry to Gay People and Their Families. Denver: Parents of Gays, 1976.

An address by the coordinator of Parents of Gays (1435 Vine Street, Apt. 6, Denver, CO 80206) presented to the Commission on Women in Ministry of the Division of Education and Ministry of the National Council of Churches.

419. Fiske, Adele M. Friends and Friendship in the Monastic Tradition. Cuernavaca, Mexico: Centro Intercultural de Documentation, 1970.

Facsimiles of articles written by a nun, each separately paginated.

420. Friends, Society of. Pacific Yearly Meeting. Working Paper on Homosexuality. Privately printed, no date. Available from Friends Book Store, 156 North 15 Street, Philadelphia, PA 19102.

421. Gay Theory Work Group of the Movement for a New Society. Gay Oppression and Liberation, Or: Homophobia, Its Causes and Cures. Philadelphia: Privately printed, 1977. Available from the Movement for a New Society, 4722 Baltimore Avenue, Philadelphia, PA 19143.

422. Griffin, Bernard Cardinal. Griffin Report. Westminster, England: Privately printed, 1956.

Roman Catholic submission to the Wolfenden Report (see No. 172).

423. Haas, Harold I. Homosexuality. St. Louis: Privately printed, 1978. Available from Christ Lutheran Seminary, 607 North Grand Boulevard, St. Louis, MO 63103.

A twenty-four-page paper by a Missouri Synod Lutheran psychologist, which has been reprinted from Currents in Theology and Mission (see No. 262).

424. Hodges, Andrew, and David Hutter. With Downcast Gays--Aspects of Homosexual Oppression. Toronto: Pink Triangle, 1974.

This forty-two-page pamphlet points out how homosexual individuals have absorbed self-hatred and hatred of their own kind from society itself and have perpetuated that oppression. "Church" and "Christians" are mentioned a number of times in the discussion. This work has been quite influential in the recent homosexual-liberation movement.

425. Kuhn, Donald. The Church and the Homosexual: A Report on a Consultation. San Francisco: Glide Urban Center, 1965.

A study sponsored by the Methodist Older Youth/Young Adult project of the United Methodist's Board of Christian Social Concerns and of the Glide Urban Center. A part of the importance of this work lies in its early date insofar as denominational studies are concerned.

426. Lauritsen, John. Religious Roots of the Taboo on Homosexuality. New York: Come! Unity Press, 1974.

This small booklet (on $8\frac{1}{2}$x11-inch pages) attributes most of the ills that have been inflicted upon the homosexual population of the world to the Judeo-Christian tradition and to organized religion generally.

427. Lucas, Donald S., ed. The Homosexual and the Church. San Francisco: Mattachine Society, 1966.

428. Methodist Church (England). Division of Social Responsibility. A Christian Understanding of Human Sexuality, A Report of a Working Party for the National Conference of the Methodist Church, June 1979.

London: Division of Social Responsibility of the
Methodist Church, 1979.

A thirteen-page report to the annual Conference of
British Methodists in June 1979. There are three
sections, the first formulating the bases of a Christian understanding of morality, the second dealing
with heterosexual relationships, and the third con-
sidering homosexuality and bisexuality. Section C10
of the report states that homosexual relationships
should be judged by the same criteria as heterosexual. Also printed in the Conference Agenda, 1979.

429. Mickley, Richard. Prison Ministry Handbook. Los
Angeles: Office of Institutional Ministry, Metropolitan Community Churches, 1980 (3d ed.). Available
from MCC, 5300 Santa Monica Boulevard, Los Angeles, CA 90029.

430. Millward, A. E. What the Bible Says to Homosexuals.
Winnipeg: Privately printed, 1978. Available from
the Council of Homosexuality and Religion, Box 1912,
Winnipeg, Man., Canada R3C 3R2.

Homosexual love is not condemned in scripture, Millward says, but sexual abuses are, whether homosexual or heterosexual. This paper has a somewhat
learned tone, but is not documented. Four very
large pages.

431. Moss, Roger. Christians and Homosexuality. Exeter,
England: Paternoster, 1977.

432. National Council of the Churches of Christ in the USA.
Resource Packet on Gay Issues and Ministry. New
York: Privately printed, no date. Available from
Professional Church Leadership, Division of Educa-
tion and Ministry, National Council of the Churches
of Christ in the USA, 475 Riverside Drive, New
York, NY 10027.

The key issue under discussion in this packet of articles and pamphlets is the question of ordination of

avowed homosexual candidates for the ministry by the
various participating denominations. The packet is
more apt to be ordered by libraries and organizations
than by individuals.

433. Nugent, C. Robert, and Jeannine Grammick, eds. A
Time to Speak: A Collection of Contemporary State-
ments from U.S. Catholic Sources on Homosexuality,
Gay Ministry, and Social Justice. Mt. Rainier,
Maryland: Privately printed, 1978. Available from
New Ways Ministry, 3312 Buchanan Street, #302,
Mt. Rainier, MD 20822.

Includes approximately fifty statements of varying
lengths. But note that some of the dignitaries quoted, such as Archbishop Krol of Philadelphia, are
testifying for full social justice for homosexual persons, which is not the same as full ecclesiastical
acceptance.

434. _____, _____, and Thomas Oddo. Catholic Homosexuals: A Primer for Discussion. Mt. Rainier,
Maryland: Privately printed, 1980 (5th ed.). Available from Dignity, Inc., Suite 11, 1500 Massachusetts
Avenue, Washington, DC 20008.

This booklet in question-and-answer format contains
information on Roman Catholic teaching, new
theological-pastoral approaches, and Church-related
ministries concerned with homosexuality. It is a
complete revision of an earlier version entitled Homosexual Catholics: A Primer for Discussion. Contains bibliography.

435. Peron, Jim. The Christian Counselor and the Homosexual Client. Glen Ellyn, Illinois: Privately
printed, 1979. Available from the author at Box
2140, Glen Ellyn, IL 60137.

A ten-page pamphlet, with bibliography, dealing with
the role of the counselor who has a homosexual client. No cure can be promised, says Peron, but the
client must be helped to deal with the guilt that may
arise in connection with the homosexuality. For reprint see No. 346.

436. _____. Homosexuality and the Miracle Makers.
Glen Ellyn, Illinois: Privately printed, 1978. Available from the author at Box 2140, Glen Ellyn, IL 60137.

A twenty-page pamphlet on the various ministries that claim to "cure" individuals of their homosexuality. Peron attempts to show that these groups achieve no lasting cures. The paper is documented.

437. Principles to Guide Confessors in Questions of Homosexuality. Washington, D.C.: National Council of Catholic Bishops, 1973.

438. Prologue: An Examination of the Mormon Attitude Towards Homosexuality. Salt Lake City, Utah: Privately printed, 1979. Available from Aeroplane Bookstore, East First South, Salt Lake City, UT 84111.

What it is like to be both Mormon and homosexual. The strongly negative attitude toward homosexuality held by the Church of Jesus Christ, Latter Day Saints, causes this Mormon author to refuse to use either his name or a pseudonym.

439. Protestant Episcopal Church in the U.S.A. Standing Commission on Human Affairs and Health. Report to the 66th General Convention, 1979. New York: The Commission, 1979. Available from The Executive Council, Episcopal Church Center, 815 Second Avenue, New York, NY 10017.

The commission was appointed to study the matter of homosexual ordinations following the 65th Convention (1976) and to make its report to the 66th Convention (1979). The report recommended that such candidates should be ordained if they are otherwise qualified; but the Convention voted only to recommend ordination if such candidates were nonpracticing in their homosexuality.

440. Salvatorian Gay Ministry Task Force. Ministry/U.S.A.: A Theological Model for Ministry to the Homosexual

Community. Milwaukee: National Center for Ministry, 1974. Available from NCM, 3517 West Burleigh, Milwaukee, WI 53210.

This booklet, which is geared to be a pastoral aid for priests working in this area, views homosexuality with understanding and is contrary to the prevailing attitude of the Roman Catholic Church. The Salvatorian Task Force is no longer in existence, but a new distributor (see above) was found for this work.

441. Seper, Franjo Cardinal. Declaration on Certain Questions Concerning Sexual Ethics. Rome: Sacred Congregation for the Doctrine of the Faith, 1975.

On premarital intercourse, masturbation, and homosexuality. All are marked as sinful and forbidden to Catholics in this document, which was issued in behalf of the Pope.

442. Smith, Don. Early Christianity and "The Homosexual." London: Quantum Jump, 1977.

Suggests that the malakos (passive partner in anal intercourse between males) of I Corinthians 6:9 is a reference to the sacred male prostitute, continuing the tradition of the kedeshim from Old Testament times. Fanciful.

443. Towards a Quaker View of Sex: An Essay by a Group of Friends, ed. by Alastair Heron. London: Friends Home Service Committee, 1963; rev. ed., 1964.

This is the classic Quaker statement. It says that "one should no more deplore 'homosexuality' than left-handedness. One can condemn or prohibit acts of course; that is another matter. But one cannot condemn or prohibit homosexuality as such." Eighty-four pages, including bibliography.

444. Treese, Robert L. Homosexuality: A Contemporary View of the Biblical Perspective. San Francisco: Glide Urban Center, 1966.

An important essay, prepared for the Consultation on Theology and the Homosexual, sponsored by the Glide Urban Center and the Council on Religion and the Homosexual in San Francisco, August 22-24, 1966. It was later included in Loving Women/Loving Men (No. 60).

445. Turnbull, John. More Than a Private Matter: Homosexuality in Perspective. Cincinnati: Forward Movement, 1980.

The blurb about this little booklet says: "Light on a subject that usually generates heat. Readers are challenged to deepest theological and personal levels to consider the implications for Church and society of so-called 'private' ethical decisions." Forward Movement publications are usually distributed in the vestibules of Episcopal churches.

446. United Methodist Church (U.S.) Board of Discipleship. Homosexuality and Families: Resource Packet for Families and Local Churches. Nashville, Tennessee: Discipleship Resources, 1979.

A packet of materials intended for use by families with gay members and especially for parents who know or wonder if their child is gay, and by church leaders who are planning ministries with such families.

447. United Presbyterian Church in the U.S.A. The Church and Homosexuality. New York: Privately printed, 1978. Available from the Office of the General Assembly, 1201 Interchurch Center, 475 Riverside Drive, New York, NY 10027.

This is the official report of the Task Force that was to make recommendations to the 190th General Assembly (1978) of the UPCUSA. The majority report recommended that the ordination of self-acknowledged practicing homosexual persons would not necessarily threaten the unity of the Church; but the Assembly did not follow this recommendation. The action that it did take is tacked on to the report.

448. Wyckliff, James, ed. In Celebration. Oak Park, Illinois: Privately printed, 1975. Available from Integrity, Box 891, Oak Park, IL 60303.

This includes papers and addresses from the first national convention of Integrity, the national society for "gay Episcopalians and their friends." Of the ninety-one pages here forty-nine are taken up by the convention's keynote address, delivered by Anglican theologian Norman Pittenger.

449. American Library Association. Social Responsibilities
      Round Table. Task Force on Gay Liberation. A
      Gay Bibliography. Philadelphia: Privately printed,
      1980 (6th ed.). Available from Barbara Gittings,
      P. O. Box 2383, Philadelphia, PA 19103.

      A selective nonfiction list of 563 items in sixteen
      pages. Books, articles, and pamphlets are grouped
      under topical headings: Law and Civil Rights, Gay/
      Lesbian Movement, Religion, Literature and the Arts,
      History and Biography, General. There are separate
      sections for Periodicals (213 titles), for Films and
      Filmstrips (which are annotated), and for Bibliogra-
      phies and Directories (i. e., other lists).

450. Bullough, Vern L., et al. An Annotated Bibliography
      of Homosexuality. 2 vols. New York and London:
      Garland, 1976.

      This is, or was, the definitive bibliography--that was
      published in book form--to date. There are 12,794
      entries. Religion and Ethics are combined to account
      for entries 5081 through 5575 at the end of Volume
      One. Those interested in works that have appeared
      in French and German through 1975 should by all
      means see this list.

451. Dignity, Inc. A Catholic Bibliography of Homosexual-

ity. San Diego, California: Privately printed, no
date. Available from Dignity, Inc., Suite 11, 1500
Massachusetts Avenue, Washington, DC 20008.

This list is not limited to Roman Catholic publications but is really ecumenical in scope. Its strongest
point, however, is that it includes entries from a
large number of periodicals that would not be very
well known to non-Catholics. The list is regularly
updated.

452. Indiana University. Institute for Sex Research. A Bib-
liography Compiled for the Institute for Sex Research.
Bloomington, Indiana: The Institute, 1980. Availa-
ble from the Institute for Sex Research Information
Service, 416 Morrison Hall, Indiana University,
Bloomington, IN 47405.

This bibliography, sold for the cost of photocopying
in segments, is the most thorough bibliography on
human sexuality available. The segments that pertain
to this topic are "Religious Sex Attitudes" (two pages)
and "Sex Ethics" (ten pages). Both books and articles are included. The cost per page is minimal.
There is no separation of homosexuality from the
larger area of human sexuality.

453. Lutherans Concerned. A Bibliography on Sexism. Los
Angeles: Privately printed, 1978. Available from
Lutherans Concerned, Box 10461, Fort Dearborn Sta-
tion, Chicago, IL 60610.

This list, compiled by Howard Erikson, contains
books and articles on homosexuality and on sexism
generally. There were about ninety entries as of
December 1978, but the bibliography is regularly updated. It is particularly geared to issues in the
churches today.

454. Parker, William. Homosexuality: A Selective Bibliography of Over 3000 Items. Metuchen, New Jersey:
Scarecrow, 1971.

This is a good list but is now somewhat outdistanced

by the two-volume work of Vern L. Bullough, et al.
(No. 450). As in the Bullough volumes, items are
numbered. For homosexuality and religion, for example, see under Books (Non-Fiction), Articles in
Books, and Articles in Religious Periodicals. See,
also, the entry immediately below.

455.   . Homosexuality Bibliography: Supplement,
1970-1975. Metuchen, New Jersey: Scarecrow,
1977.

Again, more than 3,000 items, in all fields, including religion. For a thorough search of religious
books and articles dealing with homosexuality, and
published before 1976, this volume--as well as Nos.
452 and 454 above--should by all means be consulted.

456. SIECUS. "Bibliography of Religious Publications on
Sexuality and Sex Education." SIECUS Report. Vol.
5, No. 3 (January 1977), pp. 8-9.

SIECUS Reports, regularly issued by the Sex Information and Education Council of the United States, are
well worth seeing by those who wish to keep abreast
of this field: books on homosexuality are reviewed
periodically.

457. Spence, Alex. Homosexuality in Canada: A Bibliography. Toronto: Pink Triangle, 1980. (Canadian Gay
Archives Publication Series, No. 1.)

Annotated and fully indexed, this is the first major
bibliography to deal with material by and about gay
people in Canada. It includes sections on literature,
criticism, medicine and the social sciences, homosexual periodicals, theses, films, video- and audio-
tapes, and much more. Spiral bound, paper, ninety
pages.

458. Verstraete, B. C. "Homosexuality in Ancient Greek
and Roman Civilization: A Critical Bibliography."
Journal of Homosexuality. Vol. 3, No. 1 (Fall
1977), pp. 79-89.

459. Weinberg, Martin S., and Alan P. Bell. Homosexuality: An Annotated Bibliography. New York: Harper and Row, 1972.

A hefty one-volume work. As this publication is associated with the prestigious Institute for Sex Research (founded by the late Alfred C. Kinsey) at Indiana University, we can hope that there will be an updated edition. But for materials that can bring it up-to-date, or for more up-to-date materials in general, see No. 452.

Appendix A: BIBLICAL REFERENCES TO HOMOSEXUALITY

Group One: Definite Homosexual References

[Readers should bear in mind that the numerous references to Sodom and Gomorrah in both the Old and the New Testaments are not, according to the critics, references to homosexuality, with the exception of Genesis 19:4-9, Ezekiel 16:47-50, II Peter 2:4-8, and Jude 6-7--and some even say that these are not. But in regard to these and all the references listed below, the better commentaries should by all means be consulted (see the Preface, above).]

Genesis 19:4-9
Leviticus 18:22
Leviticus 20:22
Deuteronomy 23:17-18
Judges 19:22-30
II Samuel 3:28-29 ("one who holds the spindle, " "effeminate one")
I Kings 14:24
I Kings 15:12
I Kings 22:46
II Kings 23:7
Job 36:14 (this usually does not come through in translation; but see the rendition in The New English Bible)
Ezekiel 16:47-50 (the only Old Testament reference in which Sodom is connected with the "abominations" of the Levitical references above)
Romans 1:26-27
I Corinthians 6:9-10
I Timothy 1:9-10

II Peter 2:4-8
Jude 6-7

Group Two: Homosexual References According to <u>Some</u> Critics

[Readers should note that there is no general agreement that
the references listed below are definite homosexual references. They are listed here because some critics allege
them to be definite homosexual references, or at least to contain some homosexual connotations. Again, commentaries
should be consulted.]

Genesis 9:20-25 (whatever the meaning is, it is veiled by
    textual corruption)
Genesis 39:1-6 (see, especially, the rendition of <u>The New</u>
    <u>English Bible</u>)
Deuteronomy 22:5 (if transvestism is related to the homosexu-
    al male prostitutes of Deuteronomy 23:17-18, above)
Deuteronomy 23:1 (and other references to eunuchs throughout
    the Bible, if these castrated males were indeed homosexual
    as many suspect)
Ruth 1:16-17 and 4:15 (only in the work of Jeannette Foster--
    see No. 55)
I Samuel 18-20 and II Samuel 1:26 (David-Jonathan narratives)
Isaiah 54:4-5 (if this represents repentant Israelites who had
    become the "dogs" of Deuteronomy 23:17-18--a definite
    reference, above--and here are exhorted to return to their
    native faith)
Joel 3:3 (4:3 in <u>The Jerusalem Bible</u>)
Wisdom of Solomon 16:23-26 (Apocrypha) (possibly--but not
    likely--a homosexual reference)
Matthew 8:5-13 ("boy" here appears as "slave" in Luke 7:1-
    10; but see translations of <u>The New English Bible</u> and <u>The</u>
    <u>New American Bible</u>)
John 11:3, 5 and 36; 13:23; 19:26; 20:2; 21:7 and 20 (the "be-
    loved disciple" passages)
Galatians 5:19-20 (the possible association of "fornication"
    with "idolatry," as in Romans 1:26-27, a definite refer-
    ence, above)
Ephesians 4:19; 5:3-5 and 12 (if these are references to the
    sexual libertines within certain of the Gnostic groups)
Colossians 3:5 (the possible association of "fornication" with
    "idolatry," as in Romans 1:26-27, a definite reference,
    above)
I Thessalonians 4:3-6 (if the abuse of other human beings re-
    ferred to here includes homosexuality)

Revelation 21:8 (if "dogs" here are the same as those of
  Deuteronomy 23:17-18, above)
Revelation 22:15 (if "dogs" here are the same as those of
  Deuteronomy 23:17-18, above)

Appendix B: PERIODICALS OF GAY RELIGIOUS ORGANIZA-
TIONS

[Publications listed below have been excluded from the bibliography, about which see the Preface, above. They mainly
contain news items of interest to their particular organizations. However, they occasionally contain original religious
articles as well as reprints from the larger publications, both
of which might be of interest to some researchers.]

Affirmation/Gay Mormons United Newsletter; news of the Los
Angeles chapter, plus articles of interest to gay/lesbian
Mormons: Box 46022, Los Angeles, CA 90046.

Affirmation/United Methodists for Lesbian and Gay Concerns;
national group's newsletter: c/o M. Collins, Box 775, Old
Chelsea Station, New York, NY 10011.

Apostolos; national watch on the anti-gay religious movement:
Box 2140, Glen Ellyn, IL 60137.

Bondings; Roman Catholic gay ministry newsletter: New Ways
Ministry, 3312 Buchanan, #302, Mt. Rainier, MD 20822.

Cellmate; Metropolitan Community Churches-affiliated paper
for prisoners and corrections workers: 5300 Santa Monica
Boulevard, Los Angeles, CA 90029.

Concord (formerly The Gay Lutheran); newsletter of Lutherans
Concerned, covering church-gay relations in all denomina-
tions: P.O. Box 10461, Fort Dearborn Station, Chicago,
IL 60610 (business), or c/o the Rev. Will Cain, 2033
Burgundy, New Orleans, LA 70116 (editorial).

Dignity; gay Roman Catholic newsletter for the U.S. and Canada: Suite 11, 1500 Massachusetts Avenue, Washington, DC 20005.

F.C.G.C. Newsletter; for Quaker lesbians and gay men and their friends in North America: Box 222, Sumneytown, PA 18084.

GALA Review; gay atheist league of America concerned with organized religion's attitudes toward gays: Box 14142, San Francisco, CA 94114.

The Gay Christian; international journal of gay theological issues: 5300 Santa Monica Boulevard, Los Angeles, CA 90029.

The Gay Lutheran (see Concord)

Gay Synagogue News; newsletter of Congregation Beth Simchat Torah: GPO Box 1270, New York, NY 10001.

G'vanim; bulletin of Congregation Beth Chayim Chadashim: 6000 West Pico Boulevard, Los Angeles, CA 90035.

In Unity; Metropolitan Community Churches news magazine: 5300 Santa Monica Boulevard, Los Angeles, CA 90029.

The Integer; newsletter of the Chicago chapter of Integrity but covers much news of interest to gay Episcopalians nationwide: Rev. Grant Gallup, P.O. Box 2516, Chicago, IL 60690.

Integrity Forum; newsletter of Integrity, national society for gay Episcopalians and their friends: Box 891, Oak Park, IL 60303.

More Light; news for Presbyterians concerned for lesbians and gay men: Box 46412, Los Angeles, CA 90046.

Record/Review; Evangelicals Concerned's newsletter and book/ periodical review: c/o Dr. Ralph Blair, 30 East 60 Street, New York, NY 10022.

SDA Kinship; national newsletter for gay Seventh-Day Adventists and their friends: Box 1233, Los Angeles, CA 90028.

UU Gay World; Unitarian-Universalist Gay Caucus newsletter: 479 Duboce Avenue, San Francisco, CA 94117.

United Church Coalition for Gay Concerns Newsletter; national publication for United Church of Christ gays and supporters: c/o D. Notter, 325 28 Street, San Francisco, CA 94131.

Voice of the Turtle; American Baptists Concerned gay caucus news: 158 Santa Clara Avenue, Oakland, CA 94610.

Denominational caucuses not yet publishing a newsletter are:

Axios, for Eastern Orthodox or Byzantine-rite Christians: Box 3361, Beverly Hills, CA 90212.

Gay People in Christian Science: c/o Oscar Wilde Memorial Bookshop, 15 Christopher Street, New York, NY 10014.

INDEX OF SUBJECTS

[Note that here, as in the INDEX OF AUTHORS below, numbers refer to entry, not page. Note also that "Christians" (except for denominations of Christians), "Judeo-Christian tradition," and "homosexuality" are of too frequent occurrence to index.]

303, 310, 315, 336, 337, 344, 348-353, 368, 388, 397,
401-403, 407-409, 414, 430, 442, 444, 449, 450, 454,
455
Bisexuality 74, 259, 275, 387, 428
Buggery see Sodomy

Canaan 268. See also Bible, biblical references
Canada, Canadians 430, 457
Capitalists 51
Catholic see Roman Catholic, Roman Catholics
Celibacy 42, 64, 252, 368
Celts 51
Christ 62, 128, 128a, 212, 219, 278, 285. See also Jesus
Church of England 35, 67, 70, 88, 357
Clergy 18, 37, 88, 178, 213, 272, 312, 372, 391. See also
    Ordination; Pastors, pastoral; Priests (Roman Catholic)
"Coming out" 170, 209, 229, 255, 258, 275, 276, 317, 341
Contraception 64, 441
Counseling, counselors 4, 33, 34, 37, 46, 76, 90-92, 124,
    139, 174, 244, 272, 284, 346, 366, 392, 396, 435-437
Crime, crimes 5, 177, 324. See also Law, laws (civil)

David 59, 75, 78, 82, 125, 144, 388, 403
Deuteronomy (book of) 127. See also Law, laws (Old Testa-
    ment)
Dignity 189, 234, 416, 434, 451. See also Roman Catholic,
    Roman Catholics
Disciples of Christ (Christian Church) 199, 417
Discrimination 5, 373. See also Oppression, persecution

Eastern Orthodoxy, Eastern Orthodox Christians see Ortho-
    dox, Orthodoxy (Eastern)
Education (religious) 251, 358, 363, 368, 371, 456
Emperors (Roman) 100. See also Ancients, ancient world;
    Rome, Romans
England see Church of England; Great Britain, British
Episcopal, Episcopalians 20, 21, 74, 85, 92, 120, 184, 219,
    221, 240, 247, 270, 275, 286, 358, 367, 373, 378, 439,
    445, 448
Ethics, ethical 6, 7, 14, 23, 28, 40, 71, 73, 79, 114, 122-
    124, 136, 137, 146, 152, 153, 157, 167, 187, 190, 202,
    212, 214, 231, 233, 243, 247, 250, 264, 266, 292, 313,
    333, 334, 336, 337, 386, 391, 401, 406, 411, 428, 441,
    445, 450, 452

INDEX OF AUTHORS